CIVIL SOCIETY IN THE ASIA-PACIFIC REGION

CIVIL SOCIETY
IN THE
ASIA-PACIFIC
REGION

Isagani R. Serrano

CIVICUS
World Alliance for Citizen Participation

Published by CIVICUS

919 18th Street N.W.
Suite 300
Washington, D.C. 20006
U.S.A.

ISBN 971-8817-09-3
Printed in the Philippines

CONTENTS

ACKNOWLEDGEMENTS

Many thanks go to many people and institutions whose names appear in the annotated bibliography. Many deserve more than just inclusion in a long impersonal list but they prefer not to be identified separately and are pleased enough to see their ideas faithfully reflected in the text. I hope I have satisfied their wish.

But it's hard to avoid citing a few names. Apart from the CIVICUS people who are already credited somewhere in the book, the following need special mention: Dr. W.M.K. Wijetunga, secretary-general of the Asia-Pacific Bureau of Adult Education (ASPBAE) for the steady flow of material and moral support; Horacio R. Morales, president of the Philippine Rural Reconstruction Movement (PRRM) for leading me to Rajesh Tandon and CIVICUS and giving me the encouragement, institutional backing, and space to work on this project; and my workaholic and gracious secretary, Mavic Cabigas, without whose skillful computer work my manuscripts would have been a mess.

Finally, this book should belong to its subject, the thousands of voluntary citizens' organizations whose everyday struggles are helping transform the Asia-Pacific.

PREFACE

By some accounts of history, Asia-Pacific region has been considered as the source of human civilization. It certainly contains countries with cultural civilisational records going back more than 5000 years in our history. That richness of tradition has also been reflected in various ways of organising the society, its economic enterprises and its political governance. In the last five decades, countries of the Asia-Pacific region have also demonstrated diverse approaches to social transformation, growth and development. We have had the traditions of Communist Governments in countries like China, and State-led socialist development in countries like India. The region has also had such economic giants as Japan, Korea, Taiwan and Singapore. Many states have had totalitarian regimes and Military Dictatorships. Some countries of the region have demonstrated economic advancement of rich level, others have large sections of a population living in abject poverty.

In the last two decades, the region has also witnessed enormous variety of peoples movements, social groups and voluntary development organisation. With all its diversity, Institutions of the Civil Society have survived and grown in a variety of forms and manifestations.

While various studies have attempted to document specific examples of these experiments in the Civil Society in particular countries, this is the first time that an attempt has been made to capture the flavour of these initiatives on a regionwide canvas. Inspired by the initiative of CIVICUS, this study of the Civil Society is an attempt to capture the broad trends and emerging challenges.

In no way a study of this kind can be exhaustive or deterministic. It is an evolutionary document intended to catalyze further reflections and debates, both within as well as outside, the actors of the Civil Society. It is hoped that this document can serve that purpose and thereby mobilise regionwide alliance of citizen's participation in determining their own future at this juncture of human history. We invite you to participate in this process on the basis of your own experiences and perspectives.

RAJESH TANDON
New Delhi, India

FOREWORD

This survey on the status of citizen action in the Asia-Pacific region is part of a global study conducted by CIVICUS: World Alliance for Citizen Participation. CIVICUS is an international alliance of organizations and individuals to strengthen citizen action and influence throughout the world through voluntary initiative, philanthropy and community service. The founding precept of CIVICUS is that effective societies exist in direct proportion to their degree of citizen participation and influence.

CIVICUS has as its action plan:

1. To encourage the regional and national associations whose purpose is to strengthen local efforts for involvement and impact of citizens;

2. To help establish an international climate that will provide global moral, technical and legal support to those trying to develop pluralism and empowerment in their countries and communities;

3. To become an effective international meeting ground and resource for information, models and contacts for the development of citizen involvement.

Regional reports from Europe, Asia/Pacific, Middle East, Africa, Latin America/Caribbean and North America will be used as building blocks for the World Report, which will be published in the second half of 1994. The World Report is intended to be a thought-provoking, galvanizing action-oriented study which takes stock and makes sense of the present status of the independent and voluntary sector, and highlights the problems and opportunities for citizen participation in today's world. The World Report will also be the basis for CIVICUS' first World Assembly, to be convened January 10-13, 1995 in Mexico City.

MIGUEL DARCY DE OLIVEIRA
Co-chairperson
CIVICUS

INTRODUCTION

- -

A book serves many purposes. It can inform; it can also organize people. This book tries to do both.

CIVICUS, the moving spirit behind this book, wants to share a broad picture of civil society in action among the civic actors themselves. CIVICUS is an alliance for citizen participation aiming to strengthen citizen action and influence everywhere through voluntary initiative, philanthropy and community service. It was formed in 1992 by a multinational group of civic leaders actively involved in a variety of issues affecting citizen participation in their home countries and internationally.

CIVICUS will produce a world report on the state of the voluntary sector building on reports from Asia-Pacific, Latin America, Africa, the Arab region, North America, Western Europe and Eastern Europe. The reports have been guided by the terms of reference the consultants and writers drew up together during the meeting of the CIVICUS World Report Committee in March 1993, in Budapest, Hungary.

The reports are important in the process preparatory to the CIVICUS world assembly to be held in 1995. They have introduced CIVICUS to prospective members of the emerging alliance. They will be circulated widely among those who we hope will join the world assembly.

With *Civil Society in the Asia-Pacific Region*, I hope to contribute to realizing the envisioned world report. This book is a collective product of a group organized by CIVICUS board member Rajesh Tandon, who is also president of both the Asia-Pacific Bureau of Adult Education (APSBAE) and Participatory

Research in Asia (PRIA). The third member of the group is Suneeta Dhar of PRIA. We met once during the May-June 1993 ASPBAE workshop in Sydney, Australia.

I presented the first draft of this book at the CIVICUS meeting in November 1993 in Tunis. I strengthened parts of the work based on suggestions of the meeting participants and on separate consultations with Rajesh Tandon. I wrote 19 additional illustrative stories and included an extract from *Towards Green Villages* by Anil Agarwal and Sunita Narain, published by the Centre for Science and Environment. I hope the tables, figures and annexes have further improved this book.

Writing a book based on existing literature is sometimes as difficult as doing primary research. I had to make do with what our group could collect in the brief time allotted. Unfortunately, the constraints of time did not allow me to consider all the relevant literature available.

Civil Society in the Asia-Pacific Region deals with a complex mosaic of voluntary organizations. Using the framework of challenges and responses, I try to describe the dynamic of engagement among the citizens and the state and market forces which together decide the outcomes of development processes in the region. The book reflects my own interpretation of CIVICUS' vision and I take sole responsibility for it. As I once told Rajesh Tandon, in the end a writer writes only what he wants to see and hopes the reader will identify with it.

I hope this book does justice to what CIVICUS wants itself and others to see.

Isagani R. Serrano
March 1994

CHAPTER 1

THE SUBJECT OF THIS BOOK

This book is about the voluntary associations of citizens in the Asia-Pacific region. It attempts to construct a profile of this social sector — its roots, motivations, inspirations, visions, purposes, activities, means, hardships and successes — and to evaluate its importance and contribution to social transformation, national harmony, stability and development.

Voluntary associations are groups, organizations and movements freely formed by citizens not for profit, but to advance group interests or the common good. They mediate between the private citizens on the one hand and state and corporate structures on the other. They are the building blocks of society through which individuals express a sense of belonging and develop solidarity with others.

Voluntary associations are similar to the nine independent sectors identified in *Agenda 21*, the global plan of action which emerged from the United Nations Conference on Environment and Development (UNCED) in Rio de Janeiro in 1992: women; children and youth; indigenous people and their local communities; NGOs; farmers; workers and trade unions; scientific and technical community; business and industry; and local authorities.

I do not write much about the last two sectors because they are part of either the state system or business corporations. I do consider them in so far as they affect the development of the voluntary citizens' movements, either as positive or impeding factors. I also consider other citizens groups, such as neighborhood associations, consumer societies and other voluntary organizations.

The groups that are the subject of this book are nongovernmental and non-profit. They include all voluntary groups independent of government and the business sector. They are sometimes called the "third sector" in the triadic paradigm which includes the government and business. Some writers, such as Rajesh Tandon (Annex 1), assert that the third sector should actually be the first, arguing that voluntary action preceded the state.

The third sector has a variety of names. Some call its members nongovernmental organizations (NGOs), including any citizen association not part of government or business. Others call it the independent sector. In any case, this study is concerned less with names, which I will use flexibly, than with the sector's broad defining features.

Richard Holloway, Executive Director of Private Agencies Collaborating Together (PACT) in Bangladesh, has systematically classified the three sectors. Using the images of Prince, Merchant and Citizen developed by Marc Nerfin in *IFDA Dossier*, Holloway identified how the three sectors of society — government, business, civil society — mobilize their resources (Table 1). He then constructed a detailed typology of organizations of civil society applying it to the case of Bangladesh.

Holloway says that "the fundamental distinction is between those organizations operating for the benefit of their members and those operating for the benefit of others." He further asserts that "the governance structure, the accountability, the access to resources,

Table 1. The Three Sectors of Society, by Richard Holloway

	Sector	Symbol	Primary Resource Mobilization
First	The Government Sector (incl. Armed Forces)	The Prince The Merchant	Command and Coercion
Second	The Business Sector	The Merchant	Trade and Exchange
Third	Private, Non-Profit (Civil Society)	The Citizen	Shared Values and Commitment

the links to outsiders all depend on whether the organization is a creation of its members for itself or a creation of individuals for others."

Holloway classifies organizations into three (Table 2 and Annex 2). The first class includes membership organizations or those organizations helping themselves, such as indigenous community groups, induced community groups, mass organizations, cooperatives, religious societies, trade organizations and professional organizations. The second includes non-membership organizations or those which help others, such as local philanthropic institutions, NGOs (private voluntary welfare and development organizations), area-based benevolent societies, service clubs and non-profit companies. The third are "spurious organizations" or "not helping," such as "NGOs" for personal profit, government-organized "NGOs"

Table 2. Organizations of Civil Society by Richard Holloway

A. Membership (help their members)

1. Indigenous Community Groups
2. Induced Community Groups
3. Mass Organizations
4. Cooperatives
5. Religious Societies
6. Trade Organizations
7. Professional Organizations

B. Non-Membership (help others)

1. Local Philanthropic Institutions
2. NGOs - i.e. Private Voluntary Welfare and Development Organzsations
3. Area-based Benevolent Societies
4. Service Clubs
5. Non-Profit Companies

C. Spurious (not helping)

1. "NGOs" for personal profit
2. Government-organized "NGOs"
3. Donor-organized "NGOs"
4. Business-organized "NGOs"

---

or GONGOs, donor-organized NGOs or DONGOs and business-organized NGOs or BONGOs.

Holloway's typology covers all civic organizations discussed in this book. Guided by this typology, I hope to draw a broad and vivid picture of citizens' voluntary action and its impact on development in the Asia-Pacific.

The Asia-Pacific region is a vast territory covering four subregions — South Asia, East Asia, Southeast Asia and the South Pacific. It includes some of the largest and most populous countries in the world, such as China, India and Indonesia, as well as the small island states of Micronesia, which are barely visible on the map and have fewer people than a small county in China.

Excluding the Asian part of the former Soviet Union, 50 countries comprise this region, accounting for more than half the land area and territorial waters of the globe. Their aggregate population exceeds the combined populations of Africa, Middle East, North America, Latin America and Europe.

South Asia consists of Afghanistan, Bangladesh, Bhutan, India, Iran, Maldives, Nepal, Pakistan, and Sri Lanka. East Asia includes China, Hongkong, Japan, the two Koreas, Macau, Mongolia and Taiwan. Southeast Asia includes Brunei, Myanmar (Burma), Indonesia, Kampuchea, Laos, Malaysia, the Philippines, Singapore, Thailand and Vietnam.

South Pacific is further subdivided into three groups. Micronesia consists of Guam, Kiribati, Marshall Islands, Nauru and Palau. Melanesia includes Australia, Fiji, Irian Jaya, East Timor, Kanaky (New Caledonia), Papua New Guinea, Solomon Islands, and Vanuatu. Polynesia includes American Samoa, Aotearoa (New Zealand), Cook Islands, Futuna, Hawaii, Niue, Tahiti, Tokelau, Tonga, Tuvalu and Western Samoa.

This list should evoke an appreciation of the diversity of the region's extreme historical, cultural, economic, political and geographical diversity, about which it is probably best not to generalize. Vast differences exist not only between countries, but within them.

This book cannot capture the nuances and richness of voluntary action in each country. Apart from problems of availability of and access to materials, I had to face the stark reality that so much is simply not documented. There are no precise records of the number of civic associations; no directory gives accurate figures. The UN offices, such as ECOSOC, the Nongovernmental Liaison Service and the UNCED Secretariat, have only limited information. Country inventories are not accessible and the available ones are, at best, based on guesses. The universe of our subject will probably remain unknown for a long time.

For this study, I assume that there is a huge independent sector that is growing fast. Because its exact size may never be established, I make do with what is available and extrapolate from it.

China, the biggest country in the Asia-Pacific, is a highly organized society. Both young and adult Chinese are likely to belong to one or other type of association. But it would be a researcher's nightmare to sort out the autonomous part of that organized society. Until recently, the Chinese had no clear idea of what an NGO is, at least not in the terms that it is understood elsewhere.

India, the second most populous country in Asia-Pacific, probably has the highest number of autonomous citizens' organizations, although exact figures are not available either. Aside from those frequently mentioned in development literature, there are thousands upon thousands of other local associations of citizens throughout the country.

In Japan, where the term NGO was unheard of until recently, 131 NGOs and foundations were listed in 1986. But this figure is but a tiny fraction of autonomously organized societies in the country.

Like India, the Philippines has a dynamic civil society. The country's Securities and Exchange Commission listed about 26,000 organizations in the early 1990s, from the Boy and Girl Scouts to private voluntary organizations doing development work. There are around 2,000 development NGOs.

There are around 14,000 organizations registered with the National Culture Commission of Thailand. These organizations are as diverse as those in the Philippines or Bangladesh. There are about

400 NGOs involved in development activities but not all are registered.

In smaller countries, it is much easier to get precise figures. Nepal, for example, had 1,200 NGOs and people's organizations as of 1991. Their growth is also easier to plot. From the first NGO in 1926, the number grew to no more than 100 in 1961, despite Nepal's experiment in democracy from 1951 to 1961. During authoritarian rule, 1961 to 1990, the number of organizations jumped to 400. During the the transition to multiparty democracy, the number swelled to around 1,200.

The Societies Act of Malaysia

Passed in 1966, the Societies Act of Malaysia requires all social organizations to be registered with the Registrar of the Ministry of Home Affairs. Answerable only to the Minister of Home Affairs, the Registrar exercises almost unlimited powers, including that of dissolving organizations and searches without warrant. A judge cannot intervene with the Registrar's acts and appeals can be raised only to the Minister of Home Affairs.

More than 14,000 organizations are covered by the Societies Act. These range from sporting clubs and Chinese trade guilds to consumers' associations.

The Societies Act has its roots in the British colonial period. At the end of the last century, the British colonial administration passed the Societies Ordinance to curb the powerful Chinese secret societies, the Triads. According to this Ordinance, social organizations — as well as subversive political organizations — had to be registered by the authorities.

The present Societies Act forms part of the all-embracing Internal Security Act (ISA), a draconian law enacted by the Malaysian government following the social and political unrest of the 1960s. The ISA was meant to tighten government control over social and political organizations, whether or not they were linked with the communist movement.

The political environment is a major factor in determining the number of voluntary associations in a country. The ease or difficulty of finding out exactly how many there are depends on state policies and legislations and the attitude and circumstances of citizens' groups. Where registration is not required, as in the Philippines or Thailand, many citizens' groups do not bother to register at all.

Authoritarian regimes normally demand registration of all societies, enabling governments to draw up an accurate inventory. In Malaysia, for example, the all-encompassing Societies Act of 1966 covered more than 14,000 organizations, ranging from sporting

---

In 1981, new amendments further tightened government control and sparked a massive protest against the Societies Act. Led by a broad coalition of social organizations called Conference of Societies, the protests challenged the government's definition of political and non-political organizations and the unlimited powers vested in the Registrar. The government considered political all organizations trying to influence government policy. These organizations were forbidden to have any contact with foreign organizations and to receive money from abroad.

As a result of these protests, the amendment bill was put aside but reappeared later in another form which was eventually passed by the parliament. The amended Societies Act no longer makes any distinction between political and non-political organizations. Organizations are allowed to enter into contract with foreign organizations without having prior permission from the Registrar. But they have to inform the Registrar of all their foreign financial and organizational transactions. Also, the Registrar reserves the right to forbid such contracts and transactions as well as the right to carry out searches of the organizations' premises without warrant, to remove an organization's board and to amend relevant statutes as he deems necessary.

The voluntary associations of citizens in Malaysia have continued to grow in spite of these repressive laws.

clubs and Chinese trade guilds to consumers' associations. The Indonesian government followed the same track as Malaysia when it passed the Law on Social Organizations in 1985, requiring all social organizations to register within two years of the law's passage. The extent of compliance by Indonesian organizations, however, is yet to be ascertained.

Repressive state policies and legislations pushed many citizens' groups into clandestine resistance; a good part of organized voluntary activities were and are conducted outside of legal parameters. Even during transitions from authoritarianism to multiparty democracy, many citizens' associations, especially those involved in underground activities, are reluctant to come out in full view of the public.

It is not easy to predict, describe and assess the responses of citizens to challenges facing them. The only thing certain is that they will respond to anything affecting human welfare. Citizens will engage the state and corporations and will relate among themselves according to certain norms and values and under conditions over which they may or may not have complete control.

This book is about engagement seen from the perspective of the citizens. It is about how citizens' associations and movements relate to government and other elite development actors, and among themselves.

The forms of engagement vary widely from country to country, determined by the stimulus, motivations, intentions, capacities, cultures, traditions, values and other considerations that induce citizens to come together and fight to improve their lot.

Citizens resist as well as cooperate. They fight back openly, as in mass protests, or quietly, as when they engage in footdragging, silent boycot and other forms of non-cooperation and civil disobedience. They criticize, debate, discuss, confront, advocate, promote and demonstrate alternative ways of doing things. Citizens have even brought authoritarian governments to their knees.

This book will describe the sites, forms, processes and the outcomes, both intended and unintended, of engagement. It will be difficult to avoid sweeping generalizations; the vignettes interspersed

The Law on Social Organizations in Indonesia

In 1985, despite stirrings from different Islamic leaders and organizations and NGOs, the Indonesian Parliament passed the *Undang Organisasi Kemasyakaratan* or Law on Social Organizations. Within two years after passing the law the government required all social organizations to comply with the stipulated terms. So far, everyone seems to have complied with the government's demand.

An outstanding feature of the Law on Social Organizations which caused the protestations was the obligation to adopt the *Pancasila* as the sole principle for all social organizations. Pancasila is the declared state philosophy which literally means five pillars: (a) the One and Almighty God; (b) just and civilized Humanity; (c) The Unity of Indonesia; (d) Democracy or *Kerakyatan* guided by wise policy through consultation and representation; and (e) Social Justice for all the Indonesian people. It is the guiding state ideology articulated first by Sukarno shortly before independence in 1945 and later appropriated by the New Order Government of President Suharto following the bloody events of 1965-1966.

In addition to the Pancasila, the law also provides for the compulsory registration of all social organizations, obligatory membership of these organizations with umbrella organizations, the right of the Government to "guide" and dissolve social organizations, and the control by the Government of the flow of funds from foreign donor organizations to their local Indonesian partners.

The Law on Social Organizations takes on from the so-called ORMAS Law which contains all the abovecited Pancasila articles of faith of the New Order Government. ORMAS stands for *organisasi masa* or mass organizations. No organization has the right to exist if it does not comply with the ORMAS Law.

According to the ORMAS Law, mass organizations are those with broad mass-based membership such as trade unions or the Islamic Nahdlatul Ulama and Muhammadiyah. The Law on Social Organizations speaks of "organizations established voluntarily by citizens of the Republic of Indonesia, on the basis of similarity in activity, profession, function, religion and belief in the One and Almighty God, with the purpose to participate in National Development aimed at achieving the National Goal, within the framework of the Unitary State of the Republic of Indonesia." The Indonesian government prefers the latter's all encompassing definition.

Compulsory registration and reporting was not part of the 1945 Indonesian Constitution. Only organizations opting for legality, such as the Yayasan (Foundation), have to register as required by the Court and by the Ministry of Justice. Under the Law on Social Organizations virtually no organizations are spared from such obligation.

Social organizations come under the general supervision of the Minister of Home Affairs. This responsibility is delegated to the lower level, the provincial governor or *bupati*, with respect to social organizations of subnational scope.

Social organizations can be suspended, dissolved and declared illegal for activities which the government considers to be disturbing of general security and order. These activities include the following: (a) the spread of hostility among ethnic groups, religions, races, and groups; (b) destroying the unity and integrity of the na-

throughout the book will, I hope, give flesh to the bare bones of the grand narrative.

The sources for this study were limited to literature and interviews; the pressures of time did not permit me to do primary research. But I have drawn conclusions from what is available, consistent with the perspective articulated above.

The book describes the context of Asia-Pacific development in the next chapter. Chapter 3 gives a historical overview of the emergence of citizens' organizations into the mainstream of public life. Chapter 4 describes citizens' groups in action and the shift in movement paradigms over time. Chapter 5 deals with core themes — local development and governance — the *raison d' etre* of citizens' movements which defines their location in the triadic social para-tion; (c) undermining the authority and/or discrediting the Government (d) hindering the implementation of the development programmes; and (e) other activities which may disturb political stability and security.

Similar sanctions also apply to getting aid from foreign parties without the Central Government's consent and/or rendering assistance to foreign parties detrimental to the interests of the State and Nation. Assistance from foreign parties includes finances, equipment, personnel, and facilities. Assistance to foreign parties detrimental to the interests of state and nation include those which: (a) may harm the relations between Indonesia and other countries; (b) may give rise to threats, challenges, hindrances and disturbances directed against the security of the state; (c) may disturb national stability; and (d) are detrimental to foreign policy.

The Indonesian Law on Social Organizations has much in common with the Societies Act and Internal Security Act (ISA) of Malaysia. Indeed, all three are classic examples of repressive laws informed by the national-security doctrine that guided authoritarian governments in Asia, Africa and Latin America, including part of the Western world, in the 1960s and 1970s.

❦

digm. The final chapter indicates what is in store for the citizens' struggle for participation and empowerment as Asia-Pacific moves toward the 21st century.

❦

NGOs in China

We looked out for NGOs but they were not there. Or, maybe, we just saw something different, not the kind we usually associate with the name NGO, as we know it.

This was China of March 1989. There was yet no big sign of the Tien An Men uprising which would happen a few months after. But there were stirrings in schools and factories, telling visitors that something was up in the air.

Until recently, the NGO is a concept that barely exists in the Chinese psyche. To some Chinese, the closest that comes to the definition is the Communist Party.

The civic voluntary tradition in China was broken when the communists took over in 1949. What used to be nongovernmental formations challenging the feudal lords and the Koumintang government were later transformed wholesale into organs of the new government.

China, however, has opened the door to NGO revival. A consortium of European NGOs has operated in China since 1986. Called the NGO China Group, involving Oxfam (United Kingdom), NOVIB (Netherlands), and German Agro-Action (Germany), it assists the Chinese government in reaching out to the poor.

China has one of the best records in social levelling and food security. But 70 million or 12.3 per cent of its 870 million rural population still remain under the poverty line. They are mostly minorities who live harsh lives in the barer regions of China.

To move these poor millions out of absolute poverty will require the participation of private voluntary societies. Recognizing this, the Chinese government allowed the formation of the Foundation for Underdeveloped Regions in China (FURC) in March 1989.

The anti-poverty focus of FURC is quite clear. Its NGO character, however, is a bit fuzzy. The people who compose it are a mix bunch of government and party officials and private citizens, which indicates how far NGOs in China (and there are only three to speak of as of now) have gone toward genuine autonomy from government.

Private enterpreneurship has been having a field day since the start of reform in 1978 and the NGO seems like a halfway house, not influencing policy until recently. China has nearly completely given up on the commune. Cooperatives could have been revived and allowed to develop alongside and in spite of full-scale privatization. This could have provided a solid basis for the NGO resurrection. Apparently, these were not taken into account by the policymakers.

The production responsibility system (PRS) has since been the order of the day. Emphasizing productivity and performance against the old "work-point system" which insures relative equity, the PRS has given rise to a new phenomenon of social inequality amid uneven economic growth. For example, key cities, like Beijing, now teem with unemployed putting severe pressures on the already inadequate social housing program.

Agricultural tenancy is back. Farms are up for grabs to any household or individual willing to till and make them profitable. But in China there is only one landowner, the state, which levies a specified rent on the land user.

The development process in China is so complex as to make judgement difficult. But if we were to hazard a bold one, it is that government, for four decades, has been omnipresent and overbearing and virtually left no room for private voluntary organizations.

For having assumed absolute responsibility over more than a billion people, the government has no one else to blame but itself for all the problems that later grew out of such a closed system and the choking socio-political climate that it breeds. The recent Tien An Men tragedy, just like all other tragedies that preceded it, may simply be symptomatic of a fundamental problem attending every revolution which forgets its own beginnings upon victory.

The communist party and its organized constituency were but an alternative NGO system before coming to power. Just like in other socialist countries this tradition in China seems to have the misfortune of falling victim to short memory from the moment of victory onward.

Ironically, NGOs are probably all there is in the end. So, why worry if hundreds of them bloom and contend?

CHAPTER 2

A NEW ASIAN DRAMA

- -

Two processes are shaping development in the Asia-Pacific region. The first and dominant one is regionalization from the top by states, interstate bodies and transnational corporations which seek homogenization and monopoly of resources and decisions.

The second, and the wave of the future, slowly emerging as cutting edge, is transnational democratization from below, spearheaded by voluntary associations and movements of citizens cutting across social classes. It represents diversity and horizontal spread of decisionmaking power at the grass-roots level.

The two processes are in dynamic tension. The forces that propel them clash in a sharp debate that pits the requirements of a certain kind of development against harm done to society and the environment. The issue: what constitutes equitable and sustainable development? However, conflicting processes may some day complement each other and converge to bring about enduring development.

A New Twist in Globalization

Regional powers are attempting to secure Asia for the Asians. But "Asians" to them do not mean the ordinary citizens of the Asia-Pacific who, it is true, may benefit tangentially from regionalization, but the nation-states and transnational corporations.

The world offers fewer and fewer spoils for competing nation-states and corporations. The once seemingly infinite ecological space is near congestion. The arena for capitalist competition has shrunk drastically. The rich and powerful are now locked in intense conflict over the remaining space.

This is the global context of increasing regional economic stonewalling. The US is securing North America to fend off Europe and Japan. Europe is securing its ramparts against the US and Japan. Japan is shielding Asia against the US and Europe. The three powers are operating in the tradition of partition although under circumstances different from those that gave rise to two world wars.

The Asia-Pacific region is better off than Europe or North America. As other major economies either recede or collapse, Japan enjoys a huge trade surplus, the newly industrializing countries (NICs) of South Korea, Taiwan, Singapore and Hongkong continue to boom, the near NICs of Thailand, Malaysia and Indonesia are catching up, and China is undeniably a rising powerhouse.

By sheer size of its population, the Asia-Pacific region is a huge market. On an aggregate level, the region's middle class consumers far exceed those of Europe or North America. One needs only to consider that in the biggest countries of this region, like China, India, Indonesia, Pakistan and Bangladesh, 3 out of 10 people may be considered middle class consumers of high-tech products such as cars, computers, VCRs, and color television sets.

Amid global contraction of ecological space, the Asia-Pacific region has still retained much of its rich natural resource base whose potential may yet weather a NIC-type growth for some countries and for sometime. The region's rainforests, land, freshwater and marine resources can still tolerate a degree of rapid economic growth and population pressure. Its sink capacity for human and industrial wastes is not yet exhausted.

But the region's comparative advantages are superficial and will not last long. In Asia-Pacific poverty and inequality exist side by side with affluence. Rapid exploitation is depleting its rich natural capital. Developed countries in and outside the region are eyeing it as a dumping site of industrial wastes.

Poverty and Affluence

Asia-Pacific is home to the richest and the poorest in the world. The countries which belong in this region cut across all income categories, the low, middle and high. But most of them, especially the most populous ones, are in the low-income category.

The *World Bank's 1992 World Development Report* classified the countries according to GNP per capita, using 1990 as benchmark. The 43 low-income countries (LICs) have a per capita income of $610 or less, the 58 middle-income-countries (MICs) $611 to $7,619, and the 24 high income countries (HICs) $7,620 or more. The report does not include 57 countries with populations of less than 1 million and the so-called "other economies" of the former USSR, North Korea and Cuba.

Fifteen Asia-Pacific countries belong to the low-income category: Nepal, Bhutan, Laos, Bangladesh, India, China, Pakistan, Sri Lanka, Indonesia, Afghanistan, Cambodia, Myanmar, Vietnam, Maldives, and Solomon Islands. Altogether, they account for over 2.5 billion people.

Twelve countries, with a total of over 221 million people, are in the middle-income category: the Philippines, Papua New Guinea, Thailand, Iran, South Korea, Western Samoa, Kiribati, Tonga, Vanuatu, Fiji, New Caledonia and Macau.

Eleven countries with an aggregate population of over 153 million, have made it to the elite league. Japan tops the list with a per capita income of $25,430, followed by Australia ($17,000) and New Zealand ($12,680). In a manner of speaking, these countries are the North, meaning the rich and powerful, of the Asia-Pacific region.

Three of the newly industrializing countries (NICs) also belong to the high-income class: Taiwan, Singapore and Hongkong. Brunei, American Samoa, French Polynesia, Guam and Nauru are similarly blessed.

Per capita GNP provides only a partial picture of the economy and is useful to the extent that it allows us to classify and compare countries. But the Human Development Index (HDI) of the United Nations Development Program (UNDP), certainly a more accurate and comprehensive measure of the quality of life, will no doubt expose wider variations among and within countries.

Table 3. Countries of the Asia Pacific

	Population (millions) mid-1991	Land Area (thousands of square kilometers)	Per Capita Income US Dollars 1991	Life Expectancy (years) 1990	Adult Literacy Rate (%) 1990
South Asia					
Afghanistan	—	652.1	—	42.5	29.4
Bangladesh	110.6	144.0	220	51.8	35.3
Bhutan	1.5	47.0	180	48.9	38.4
India	866.5	3,288.6	330	59.1	48.2
Iran	57.7	1,648.0	2,170	662.	54.0
Maldives	0.22	0.3	460	62.5	95.0
Nepal	19.4	141.8	180	52.2	25.6
Pakistan	115.8	796.1	400	57.7	34.8
Sri Lanka	17.2	65.6	500	70.9	88.4
East Asia					
China	1,149.5	9,561.1	370	70.1	73.3
Hongkong	5.8	1.04	13,430[9]	77.3	90.0
Japan	123.9	377.8	26,930	78.6	99.0
South Korea	43.3	99.02	6,340	70.1	96.3
North Korea	23.0	120.5	—	—	—
Macau	0.5	0.02	6,455		
Mongolia	2.3	1,565	1,729	62.5	93.0
Taiwan	20.7	35.2	7,067		
South East Asia					
Indonesia	181.3	1,904.3	610	61.5	81.6
Lao PDR	4.3	236.8	220	49.7	54.0
Malaysia	18.2	329.8	2,520	70.1	78.4
Philippines	62.9	300.0	740	64.2	89.7
Singapore	3.0	0.6	14,210	74.0	88.0
Thailand	57.2	513.1	1,570	66.1	93.0
Vietnam	67.7	332.0	—	62.7	87.6
Brunei	0.4	5.8	7,681	73.5	86.0
Kampuchea	7.1	181.0	84	—	—
Myanmar (Burma)	42.8	676.6	—	—	—

	Population (millions) mid-1991	Land Area (thousands of square kilometers)	Per Capita Income US Dollars 1991	Life Expectancy (years) 1990	Adult Literacy Rate (%) 1990
South Pacific					
Micronesia					
Guam	0.12	0.55	14,303	—	—
Kiribati	0.68	0.73	732	—	—
Marshall Is.	0.04	0.17	—	—	—
Nauru	0.01	0.02	18,111	—	—
Palau (Belou)	—	0.49	—	—	—
Melanesia					
Australia	17.3	7, 686.9	17,050	76.5	99.0
Fiji	0.77	18.3	1,624	64.8	87.0
Kanaky	0.17	19.1	—	—	—
Papua New Guinea	3.64	462.8	926	54.9	52.0
Solomon Is.	0.33	28.9	588	69.5	24.0
Vanuatu	0.17	12.2	782	69.5	67.0
Irian Jaya					
Polynesia					
American Samoa	0.04	0.2	4,419	66.5	92.0
Aoteoroa	3.40	268.7	12,350		
Cook Island	0.02	236.5	—	—	—
Futuma	—	—	—	—	—
Hawaii	—	—	—	—	—
Nive	—	—	—	—	—
Tahiti	0.2	—	7,026	—	—
Tokelau	—	0.01	—	—	—
Tonga	0.1	0.7	922	—	—
Tuvalu	0.01	0.03	556	—	—
Western Samoa	0.2	2.9	626	—	—

Consolidated from the following sources: *World Development Report 1993; World Development Report 1992; Asian Development Bank Annual Report 1992; Human Development Report 1993; Third World Guide 93/94.*

Sri Lanka, for example has a low per capita income but one of the best qualities of life by HDI standards. On the other hand, Nauru, the world's smallest independent republic with 10,000 inhabitants, has one of the world's highest per capita income, but produces a single product, phosphate, and imports everything else. There is much more to good quality of life than just high income although with it one can buy good food, shelter, health, education, freedom of movement and the labor of others.

Asia-Pacific embraces five of the most populous nations in the world and is home to most of the world's more than 1 billion absolutely poor. China, India, Indonesia, Pakistan and Bangladesh have 2.4 billion people. At least half of the world's core poor lives in these countries, trying to survive on $1 a day, the standard of living in the US several generations ago.

Most of the poor live in the villages of the uplands, agricultural plains and coastal fishing grounds. They are the small and landless peasants, indigenous peoples and artisanal fishers who depend mainly on cultivating primary resources.

Asian rural life is fused to the global economic order. Products of the forests, land, freshwaters and the ocean find their way into the international market. Conversely, industrial products from the rich countries penetrate the remotest areas of rural Asia.

Challenge of Rapid Modernization

The Asia-Pacific citizen is in the eye of a whirlwind of rapid growth which may set the pace for all developing countries of the South.

Growth now means becoming a NIC. The spectacular success of South Korea, Taiwan, Singapore, and Hongkong is held up as an "economic miracle" and *the* model for all struggling economies of the South. Growth the "NIC way" is the new orthodoxy.

The story of the NICs is a grand narrative about growing first — at any price — and paying the social and ecological costs later. Common welfare, social justice, equity, and environmental health are dispensable. And here lies the biggest negative lesson of the NIC experience: growth which postpones the payment of costs to society and the environment cannot endure. It is much more expensive and difficult to clean up the mess later than to invest in its prevention from the beginning.

The NICs did in 30 years what took more than a century in the West. If the rest of Asia follows suit, the social and ecological problems now plaguing the NICs will be magnified several times.

Rapid growth will transform the Asia-Pacific from a basically agrarian region into a largely metropolitan one. By 1990, about 30 percent of this region's inhabitants lived in cities, compared to 18 percent in 1960. Growing by the rate of 3.9 percent annually from 1960 to 1990, or by 19 million people yearly, the urban population is now 849 million. Expected to grow by 3.3 percent annually in the next 30 years, the urban population, which by then will make up over half the region's entire population, will exceed 2 billion by the year 2000.

Big cities have mushroomed at an alarming rate. In 1950, there were only 19 cities with a population of one million or more. By 1970, there were 49. In 1990, there were 86 cities: 38 in China and 24 in India. By the year 2000, 12 of the world's 21 megacities will be found in this region. Bombay, Calcutta and Shanghai will each have more than 15 million people and nine other cities will have more than 10 million. Many other cities already have populations greater than 3 million, and they continue to grow rapidly.

According to an Asian Development Bank (ADB) study, the immediate reasons for rapid urbanization are natural population growth and rural-urban migration. In the past two decades, natural population growth accounted for 55 percent of the region's urban growth while the rest was due to rural-urban migration. There are variations from country to country: natural growth accounts for more than half the urban population increases in India, Malaysia, Pakistan, Philippines and Vietnam, but rural-urban migration is the key factor in countries like Bangladesh, China, Indonesia, South Korea and Thailand.

Although population growth is crucial, the rural-urban divide is the more fundamental reason for rapid urbanization. The rural-ur-

Total and Urban Population in the Asia-Pacific Region

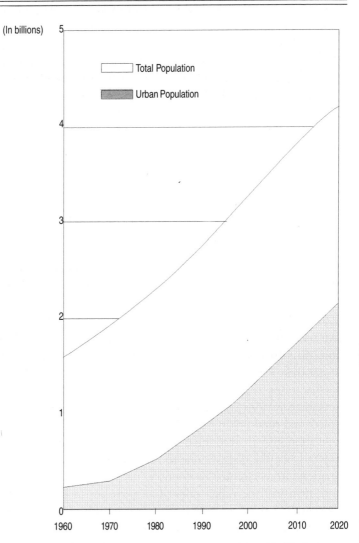

Source: Based on the Asian Development Bank's *Key Indicators for Developing Asia and Pacific Countries* and the United Nation's World *Urbanization and the Prospect for 1990.*

ban divide is rooted in an urban-biased development paradigm which defines progress as the subordination of agriculture to industry. The city is the symbol, even if an illusory one, of prosperity. It offers jobs, money, comfort, information and education. The city *is* culture; the village is lack of it. To live in the city is to have more choice.

The population explosion anticipated in Asia in the next century cannot be prevented by current population-control programs. The best way to reduce population growth is by creating the social conditions that reduce poverty and inequality and enhance the status of women. This has been proven in the cases of China, Sri Lanka and Kerala state in India. All three rank high in the UNDP Human Development Index.

China's one-child program succeeded as long as the majority of Chinese enjoyed secure land tenure, adequate education and health services and relative food security, along with guaranteed retirement benefits for old people and enhanced social status for women. However, China's birth rates have risen since 1980 after the government embarked on an aggressive modernization program that undermined previously guaranteed social safety nets. Now many Chinese once again see having more children as a means to survive in the new economic system.

In Sri Lanka, the fertility rate was brought down by nearly 40 percent between 1960 and 1985. The population growth rate averaged 1.4 percent in the first half of the 1980s. Kerala showed almost the same performance in the same period. Both cases can be explained by government's strong commitment to social welfare which greatly reduced the need of the poor to have many children in order to improve their economic position and guarantee old-age security. In addition, greater education and work opportunities for Sri Lankan and Keralan women have resulted in greater control over their reproductive life.

Success in controlling population growth cannot be sustained without a corresponding reduction in the high consumption of the rich. For example, Japan, which is considered to have exceeded its Malthusian limit of 30 million people long ago, is now a country of

Table 4. Urbanization Indicators By Country

	Urban Population (thousands)			% of Population in Urban Areas			Urban Population Growth Rate (%)	
	1960	1990	2020	1960	1990	2020	1960-90	1990-2020
NIEs								
Hong Kong	2,739	5,507	6,322	89	94	97	2.4	0.5
Korea, Rep. of	6,929	30,794	45,172	28	72	88	5.1	1.3
Singapore	1,634	2,723	3,290	100	100	100	1.7	0.6
Subtotal	*11,302*	*39,024*	*54,784*	*38*	*76*	*90*	*4.2*	*1.1*
SOUTH ASIA								
Afghanistan	861	3,021	13,617	8	18	36	4.3	5.1
Bangladesh	2,644	19,005	83,984	5	16	38	6.8	5.1
Bhutan	22	81	463	3	5	16	4.4	6.0
Myanmar	4,189	10,316	29,814	19	25	43	3.0	3.6
India	79,413	230,269	648,265	18	27	47	3.6	3.5
Nepal	292	1,837	8,878	3	10	27	6.3	5.4
Pakistan	11,042	39,250	131,802	22	32	53	4.3	4.1
Sri Lanka	1,772	3,679	9,126	18	21	39	2.5	3.1
Subtotal	*100,235*	*307,458*	*925,949*	*17*	*26*	*46*	*3.8*	*3.7*
SOUTHEAST ASIA								
Indonesia	14,032	56,293	151,036	15	31	55	4.7	3.3
Malaysia	2,053	7,701	18,479	25	43	65	4.5	3.0
Philippines	8,350	26,602	65,707	30	43	62	3.9	3.1
Thailand	3,302	12,609	35,346	3	23	45	4.6	3.5
Subtotal	*27,737*	*103,205*	*270,568*	*18*	*32*	*56*	*4.5*	*3.3*
ECONOMIES IN TRANSITION								
Cambodia	559	959	3,511	10	12	26	1.8	4.4
China	124,892	380,803	927,185	19	33	63	3.8	3.0
Lao PDR	73	770	3,263	8	19	41	5.1	4.9
Mongolia	342	1,145	2,936	36	52	66	4.1	3.2
Viet Nam	5,107	14,600	47,306	15	22	43	3.6	4.0
Subtotal	*131,073*	*398,277*	*984,201*	*19*	*33*	*61*	*3.8*	*3.1*
SMALL ISLAND NATIONS								
Cook Islands	6	4	7	33	22	41	1.3	1.9
Fiji	117	300	608	30	39	56	3.2	2.4
Kiribati	7	24	46	17	36	58	4.2	2.2
Maldives	10	63	218	11	29	53	4.2	2.2
Papua New Guinea	51	613	2,342	3	16	34	8.6	4.6

	Urban Population (thousands)			% of Population in Urban Areas			Urban Population Growth Rate (%)	
	1960	1990	2020	1960	1990	2020	1960-90	1990-2020
Solomon Islands	11	34	176	9	11	26	3.8	5.6
Tonga	12	19	36	18	20	40	1.5	2.2
Vanuatu	6	41	152	9	26	50	6.6	4.5
Western Somoa	21	37	69	19	22	40	1.9	2.1
Subtotal	*241*	*1,135*	*3,654*	*9*	*20*	*38*	*5.3*	*4.0*
TOTAL	**270,588**	**849,099**	**2,239,156**	**18**	**30**	**54**	**3.9**	**3.3**

Based on the Asian Development Bank's *Key Indicators of Developing Asian and Pacific Countries* and the United Nation's *World Urbanization Prospects, 1990.*

about 130 million people enjoying one of the world's highest living standards and most stable environments. But this prosperity and ecological stability has been achieved at the expense of many poor countries. Japan ceased to be self-sufficient in food long ago. Its industries are being fed with raw materials almost entirely coming from the outside. Its backyard is relatively clean because it dumps most of its waste in other backyards.

Rapid modernization will transform every facet of Asia-Pacific. Every country, big or small, will be fused to this inexhorable process. The leaders of the band — Japan, China and the NICs — will set the tempo of the march into the 21st century. They can already control the region's life support systems and transform the Asia-Pacific into a tight and homogenous whole at their beck and call.

This is the new Asian drama; everybody is an actor. Ordinary citizens on this side of the world stage will have to fight to define their role in the unfolding of what could turn into a tragi-comedy.

CHAPTER 3

FROM THE MARGINS
TO THE MAINSTREAM

A large number of citizens are active players in the unfolding Asian drama. Many belong to citizens' movements which challenge the dominant structures and processes, aspiring to build a future for Asia-Pacific different from that envisioned by the elite.

Major events of the past two decades indicate that those citizens movements have emerged from the margins to the mainstream of social, political, economic and cultural life. An accounting of the movements' achievements as well as debacles reveals a net progress in the struggles to broaden the centers of power.

From 1970 to 1990, authoritarian regimes in Asia fell one after the other. The toppling of the Marcos regime in the Philippines in 1986 is an archetype of people power. The feats of the people of Iran, South Korea, Thailand, Bangladesh, Nepal in deposing dictators are comparable. The democratic challenges in countries like China, Taiwan, Mynamar (Burma) and elsewhere are equally noteworthy.

In all these transitions, citizens movements played a central role. Citizens, through their voluntary associations or spontaneous participation, have demonstrated how much their collective strength can do. They can do more than just help themselves: they can also resist and bring their power to bear on the state and even bring down unaccountable governments.

Beginnings of Voluntary Action

The free associations of citizens in Asia have a long and rich tradition which harks back to precolonial communal societies. The tradition has been shaped by colonialism and modernization as well as the people's natural inclination to organize themselves.

A variety of associational forms throughout Asia Pacific has emerged and developed through time. Some, such as the communal organizations of indigenous peoples, remain distinctly Asian. Others, like trade unions and NGOs, are clearly of Western origin. Still others, like cooperatives, fuse indigenous self-help groups and Western-type cooperative institutions.

Civil society is a concept alien to Asia. It refers to self-organization of citizens in contrast to state or government and is rooted in Western rational tradition and political culture. The concept of citizenship, which suggests who are included and who are excluded in public affairs, is also a modern one. These two concepts are not foreign to some modern societies like Australia, Hongkong, Singapore and, to a certain extent, the Philippines. But they may be more alien in modern Japan, for example, which is more Asian than Western despite its high level of modernization.

Asiatic societies are largely communitarian and integrative while modern Western societies tend to be atomistic and differentiated. For good or ill, the family, the clan, the community are valued highly by Asians. A high premium is put on obedience, loyalty and respect for authority. Japanese corporations, for instance, are organized and run like a huge family and patronage runs political parties and governments. In India, the distinction between government and non-governmental institution at the local level is blurred because they form part of a unified social structure.

Voluntary action is deeply rooted in Asian communities. It is directed toward common concerns that cannot be adequately addressed by individual families and extended kinship support systems: production, exchange, rituals from birth to death, and collective security, all of which maintain community consensus and cohesion.

The most common form of organization is the self-help and mutual-exchange group. In Indonesia, the *gotong royong* or mutual help is equivalent to *bayanihan* in the Philippines. Funeral associations, of which there are thousands in Thailand, are also mutual-benefit societies.

Communal organizations ensure sound management and sustainable use of the commons, such as forests and watersheds, hunting and fishing grounds, water, sacred areas, places of worship and festivities, and so on. The present generation has inherited the rich tradition of indigenous organization and principles of natural-resources management.

One principle is *sovereignty*. Communities who live off a natural-resource base have the greatest stake in its conservation. They reserve the basic right to control, exploit, manage and benefit from it. Conversely, abuse of the right either by the local inhabitants themselves or by outsiders often results in overexploitation of resources at the expense of the community and the ecological system.

Ecosystem is another essential organizing principle in natural-resources management. Indigenous peoples and local communities have proven their capacity to live in accordance with the limits of their environment. They retain a reverence for nature; trees, rivers, stones and animals have spiritual value. In their holistic animistic view, as opposed to the anthropocentric, nature is not subordinated to human desire.

Traditional practices that have stood the test of time are compatible with these principles of sustainable development. The Cordillera peoples in the northern highlands of the Philippines, for example, replace every tree they cut with two seedlings. Giving back to nature is a common indigenous practice all over Asia-Pacific.

Even swidden agriculture, or slash-and-burn farming, now thought to be destructive of the upland ecosystem, was once sustainable. Indigenous peoples and upland farmers, with their deeply ingrained understanding of ecospace, were guided by the regenerative cycle of a tree, leaving the first clearing untouched untill second growth forests matured. If swidden agriculture has become unsustainable it is because of the massive commercial degradation of the forests and upland ecosystems and because of population pressures.

The tragedy of the commons, where everyone optimizes short-term private gain, has nothing to do with indigenous practice. The sad scenario described by Garett Hardin in his essay, "The Tragedy of the Commons," was created by greed which has destroyed the environment and eroded communal cohesion.

The Rise of Social Movements

The growth of voluntary organizations and movements can be traced back to the last 200 years, from colonial times to independence and after.

Colonialism and modernization undermined indigenous social relations and philantrophy. Colonialism wrested from the subject peoples their sovereign right over natural resources and vested it in the state. It linked far-flung rural villages to the global centers of economic and political power. Modernization built on colonial domination and pushed globalization to the limit.

Most of Asia-Pacific, with the possible exception of Thailand, was colonized by Europe and North America. Centuries of popular resistance created modern nation states. One of the first democratic republics was established in the Philippines at the turn of the 20th century. Most Asian democracies and independent governments were established after the WWII. Colonialism persists to this day but mainly in the island states of the South Pacific.

Social movements have always been at the base of independence struggles. While they cut across social classes, participants were mainly from the peasantry, the indigenous peoples, the workers, the women and the poor. The leaders were almost always from the educated middle classes. Social action and political leadership were integrated in the beginning but later separated into autonomous institutional entities once the nation state was established. The same pattern of fusion and separation was seen in post-WWII revolutionary movements which swept across all of Asia.

From this brief historical sketch we can abstract certain patterns that shaped civil society. The first was the stubborn assertion of precolonial forms of social organizations against those Western. The second was the assertion of autonomy of social voluntary action against hegemonic state agenda represented by governments-in-waiting, or the political parties or instruments for state power and governance.

What ensues from the dynamic interplay of these historical patterns will have a profound impact on the solution to global problems. The raging development-versus-environment debate has highlighted the need to establish institutions that will create a sustainable global order. It has also started a return to the wisdom of premodern societies and sparked the rethinking of the myriad forms of social organization in furthering the common good.

Western colonial powers, no matter their different styles and impacts, tried to mold Asian peoples in their image. They spread their religions, philosophies, values, lifestyles, languages, forms of government, social institutions; they subordinated native cultures and organizations. Combining force and persuasion, they induced native subjects to forget their cultural roots.

The results of the long process of colonialism varied from country to country. Societies with stronger and longer traditions, such as China and Japan, proved more resilient and more successful than others in keeping their cultures intact. Other societies succumbed much more easily, thereby losing much of their cultural anchors. Still others managed to fuse endogenous forms with externally introduced ones. However, nothing is ever completely lost; while institutions were radically transformed, indigenous cultures slumbered in the hearts and minds of the people, waiting for the historical opportunity to reassert themselves.   •

Paradoxically, intentional actions often produce unintended consequences. Instruments of subjugation became instruments of emancipation. Western ideals inspired massive participation in liberation struggles and democratic movements from the turn of the century on.

Social movements emerged before and after the two world wars. Although well rooted in local conditions and oppression, the movements were to a great extent Western-inspired. The ideals and symbols came directly from the Enlightenment and the Jeffersonian tradition, expressed in slogans like democracy, liberty, freedom and equality. The institutional forms were derived from Western democracy, like political parties, trade unions, peasant organizations, the women's emancipation movement, suffrage groups, free-thinkers societies, mutual aid societies, academic-freedom associations and so on. As is typical in highly stratified societies, an institution corresponded to almost every social concern. Western civil society was transplanted to Asia.

And yet tradition died hard. Native symbols and forms suffused the borrowed ones, integrating all external influences. Asians embraced the symbols and ideals as their own and turned them into powerful instruments against their oppressors.

States and governments which arose out of the independence struggles became the new targets of social mobilization and voluntary action and the new symbols of oppression, perpetuating the colonial legacy of poverty and inequality.

Instead of becoming a region of peace and prosperity, postwar Asia-Pacific became a center of Cold War conflict much like Africa and Latin America. The decades following WWII saw political turmoil and revolutionary upheavals rooted in unresolved issues of landlessness and poverty. In the 1960s it became clear that authoritarian development would be the typical elite response to social unrest. By the 1970s most countries were under dictatorship.

For four decades Asians were torn between authoritarian development and revolution. Social movements and citizen action galvanized by this contradiction chose revolution.

The Vietnam War was a watershed. Powerful peace movements flowered and a whole generation of young people demanded an end to the war. Many leaders of today's social movements trace their initiation into activism to that period.

The NGO Phenomenon

The importance of nongovernmental organizations (NGOs) in the operations of civil society has grown in recent years. The widespread disappointment with the outcomes of a succession of development decades, beginning from the 1960s, has triggered a search for causes and alternative solutions to the persisting problems of poverty, inequality, participation, civil conflicts and resource degradation. Governments have come under heavy criticism for their top-down approach to development, among other misdeeds. In contrast, NGOs have a bottom-up perspective, efficient service delivery, flexibility and strategic methodologies that empower the poor and excluded.

Nothwithstanding the myths and realities surrounding the NGOs, their outreach is decidedly significant. The 1993 Human Development Report says that NGO activity "touched" the lives of 100 million people in developing countries in the early 1980s. More than half of this number — 60 million people — lived in Asia. By 1993, according to UNDP estimates, the number was probably near 250 million.

Development assistance passing through the NGO system has been estimated by UNDP to have risen from $1 billion in 1970 to $7.2 billion in 1990 (official development assistance in 1990 stood at $55 billion). Of the $7.2 billion, about $5 billion was raised from private contributions of the citizens in developed countries.

NGOs may be small, tightly knit local organizations dealing with a single issue or a wide spectrum of issues covering human rights, development and environmental concerns. In recent years, NGOs have formed into national federations and international networks, building extensive linkages that give them a strong voice in national and international affairs.

In Asia-Pacific, many NGOs have grown out of people's organizations. Some of them owed their beginnings to social action inspired by Christian churches, Catholic as well as Protestant. Others have been formed by like-minded citizens wanting to respond to some human welfare issues affecting themselves or the public at large.

Many NGOs work in partnership with grassroots organizations, offering a package of political, technical, material and spiritual support. This type of NGO stresses empowerment of the poor and marginalized. Their involvement in social awareness-raising, community organizing, livelihood, health and other projects enhances popular power. Other NGOs limit their activities to advocacy for or against certain state policies that affect the citizens. The positive outcomes of their work complement the bottom-up empowerment process.

NGOs are a form of private voluntary organizations (PVO). First used by the United Nations in 1953, the term NGO refers to those non-state organizations that interface with the UN agencies and serve as their sounding boards. From then on, the term began to mean any voluntary formation not part of government, including all those that are part of social movements.

The loose meaning of the word invites confusion and objection. In some parts of India, NGO evokes negative images of development workers who channel public resources into projects at the expense of those who need them most and who glide around the villages in their flashy cars selling "development". More positively, the NGO is distinct from other voluntary organizations because it is composed of volunteer or paid career professionals who serve the poor and influence public policy.

Serving the poor means building people's capacities to take control of their own development, to alleviate poverty and misery, and to test and promote development alternatives. Influencing public policy includes monitoring and criticizing policies and activities of state and other development institutions and corporate entities to ensure that they are accountable to the people they affect. It also includes advocacy of development alternatives.

As voluntary associations of citizens with a stake in development, NGOs have the same right to exist as any other organization. That they have become the apple of the donor agencies' eye is not their fault. However, problems arise when they abuse their position, undermine the autonomy of people's organizations and act like political parties or governments.

NGOs in Asia do not exist apart from the social movements of which they are but a small part. With their increasing number and importance, NGOs continue to perform a complementary but necessary role in social transformation.

Overseas Voluntary Aid Community

Throughout modern development history, Asia-Pacific has been a huge area for international voluntary action. In the beginning, there were the Christian missions. Through their charitable, educational and evangelical activities, they served as conduits for the transfer of Western knowledge, cultures, values and technologies into a region dominated by the influences of animism, Islam, Buddhism, Hinduism and other religions.

Then came the big international NGOs. Some of the well-known names include Oxfam, Action Aid, Save the Children, World Vision, Plan International, CARE, Ford Foundation, all of which maintain a presence in the region to this day.

Within Asia-Pacific, Australia is the only country that followed the Western tradition of international voluntary work. Before WW II, international aid was pioneered by Australian Christian missions, charities and service societies. After WW II overseas aid activities dramatically increased along with the rapid growth of Australian NGOs. The 1950s saw the formation of The Lutheran World Service (1950), the Food for Peace Campaign, later to become Community Aid Abroad (1953), the Australian Baptist World Aid (1959) and the Quaker Service Australia (1959). In the 1960s more were established: For Those Who Have Less (1962), Australian Catholic Relief (1964), World Vision of Australia (1966), and the Australian Foundation for the Peoples of the South Pacific (1967).

The Australian NGOs put in $90 million to the total annual aid kitty of $5.5 billion raised by northern citizens as private contributions to programs and projects in developing countries. They also serve as channels for official development assistance.

More important, the Australian NGOs have been some of the most active in rethinking the nature and impact of development assistance and in challenging conventional development wisdom.

The South Asian BINGOS

From the highlands of Nepal and across Bangladesh, Bhutan, Pakistan, Iran and Afghanistan, down to the Indian subcontinent and all the way to Sri Lanka, thousands of NGOs are changing the lives of over a billion people. Their sizes in terms of staff, budget and scale of operations vary from small (such as Participatory Research in Asia or PRIA of Dr. Rajesh Tandon), medium (such as AWARE of P.K.S. Madhavan; PROSHIKA of Faruque Ahmed) to the truly big NGOs (BINGOs) like Sarvodaya of Dr. A.T. Ariyaratne and BRAC of F.H. Abed.

The last two examples stand out as the biggest NGOs in Asia and, probably, in the whole world.

Founded in the late 1950s by the charismatic A.T. Ariyaratne, the Sarvodaya Sharamadana Movement (SSM) has more than 7,700 staffers and covers 8,000 villages — a third of all villages in Sri Lanka — in both the Singhalese and Tamil regions of the country. SSM is inspired by Buddhism and the works of Ghandi.

Sarvodaya's long-term goal is to build democracy from below. It focuses its work on the low-caste families hoping that they can be integrated into the mainstream of public life.

SSM runs a variety of economic projects, including batik and sewing shops, machine shops and carpentry, printing press and other income-generating activities for the farmers. Its welfare programmes address the needs of the deaf and disabled, preschool children, and victims of ethnic conflicts. It helps people mobilize their own resources, especially their labor, through forms of participation and self-reliance attuned to the country's cultural traditions.

In recent years, Sarvodaya has taken a high profile in national affairs with Ariyaratne on the lead. It has openly challenged official development policies and reached out to the other sectors such as lawyers, the police, the judiciary, the media and various action groups. Ariyaratne and Sarvodaya have become important players in Sri Lankan politics.

The Bangladesh Rural Advancement Committee (BRAC) is almost as big as Sarvodaya with about 6,000 staffers and activities covering around 15,000 of the total 68,000 villages of Bangladesh. This is a tremendous achievement from its modest beginnings from February 1972 when a small group of committed people organized BRAC and started work among the refugees in the Sulla district following the country's war of liberation.

From relief and rehabilitation, BRAC soon turned to concerns and activities of a more structural nature. These cover a broad spectrum: institution building; non-formal and functional education; primary education; health education; family planning; the development of some basic clinical health services through paramedics at the village level; legal awareness; savings and credit around which are woven several other activities.

By 1992 BRAC's integrated rural development program which is being carried out through its 217 area offices covering 14,974 villages, has produced 22,361 village organizations with a total membership of nearly 800,000 of which women account for 65 percent. Credit disbursement amount to $47 million with repayment rates of 97-98 percent. BRAC has set up 9 training centers and 8,666 ongoing schools run by 7,708 teachers for 262,980 students. Its Oral Rehydration Therapy (ORT) teaching program has reached 13 million households nationwide after 10 years, a feat in a country where 250,000 children die of dehydration from diarrhea every year.

The need to scale up NGO impact is probably the single biggest justification for the emergence of the BINGOs. Now in the centerstage of NGO discourse, the question of impact has yet to put to rest the issue of appropriate size since a number of other strategic options for achieving the same purpose have now entered the debate.

CHAPTER 4

VOLUNTARY ACTION IN ASIA-PACIFIC

- -

Asians hold up half the sky, to borrow Mao's image. With a population close to 3 billion, the Asia-Pacific region will probably make or unmake the fate of humanity. It is impossible to describe in detail how so many people are organized, what inspires them to voluntary action, and what impact their actions have on their societies.

Standing between established institutions (government, churches, corporations) and the individual is a vast number of voluntary groups that shape society. Their magnitude and quality will probably never be fully known. I simply hope to paint in broad strokes some of the key movements and burning issues that push them to change society. And as I do not pretend to be able to identify the myriad groups in more than 50 countries in the region, I will focus on social movements which serve both as lodestones for the individual will and as counterpoints to established institutions.

Citizens' movements in the Asia-Pacific are complex. Their histories, motives and visions, members and leaders, and their organizing themes vary from country to country. However, the issues they put forward allow us to identify them and to map and assess their strengths, weaknesses and impact.

Voluntary action and the social movements it generates cluster around issues of rights, development and environment. These broad themes are expressed by movements of indigenous peoples, peasants, fisherfolk, trade unions, youth, women, peace and human-rights advocates, NGOs, voters, consumers and environmentalists.

These movements address multiple and interlinked crises of participation, equity and justice, civil conflicts, poverty and environmental degradation.

Changing Social-Movement Paradigms

In Asia as in other parts of the so-called Third World, social and voluntary action have been most powerfully influenced by the idea of revolution. Inspired by the struggles of Asian peoples against colonialism, explicitly revolutionary mass movements have swept across the region for a great part of the 20th century. Their ideological roots are Western and dominantly Marxist or socialist.

If the collapse of socialism in Eastern Europe and the former Soviet Union has weakened orthodox revolutionary projects, the idea of socialism has not ceased to inspire revolution. The reason is simple: social reforms continue to fall short of expectations, and problems of rights, development and environment continue to fester while the means to solve them remain inadequate.

Successful and failed revolutions in the Asia-Pacific region have been based on alliances of peasants, workers and youth, usually led by a proletarian party. The peasants produced the mass membership and most of the guerillas who together mobilized the rural masses. The workers, considered by revolutionary orthodoxy as the advanced forces of production, were the leading class. The youth and students, because of their special position in society, sparked the revolutionary prairie fire.

The paradigm holds sway to this day. Even the more recent form of voluntary organization, the NGO, cannot quite part from tradition, and continues to support grass-roots movements of peasants, workers and communities.

Asian grass-roots movements, whether of the old or evolving paradigm, have never been homogenous. Agrarian movements existed long before socialism and other ideologies were introduced to the region by colonialism. Various sectors, including government, organize peasants. The results are as diverse as the grass-roots groups themselves.

The Australian Aborigines

Tracing civilization's roots as far back in time as possible has acquired increasing significance in light of the sharpening development-versus-environment debate. It seems that indigenous peoples hold some of the clues to the outstanding questions of modern times.

In Australia, the world's biggest inhabited island and the smallest continent, there existed a culture rich and diverse in its customs, language and religion, preceding by several centuries the civilizations in the Middle East, China and Europe. For over 40,000 years before Captain Cook set foot on "The Great South Land" in 1770, more than 300,000 Aborigines inhabited the riversystems, coastal plains, mountains, tropical rainforests and drylands and deserts of this continent. They spoke 500 languages grouped into 31 related language families that were as rich and complex as the modern European languages.

The white colonizers found Australia's environment largely as it was 400 centuries before, thanks to the Aborigines' way of life. The Aboriginal traditions were built in harmony and close spiritual bond with every living thing and even with inanimate things such as rocks, rivers, the wind and others. The Aborigines regard themselves, nature and the land as inseparably bound and interdependent. It is this culture of integrity with nature that probably kept environmental degradation to a minimum.

The Aborigines are linked to what is called mythology of dreaming, or Dreamtime, which is the basis of all traditional thinking and practice. Dreamtime is the Aborigines' historical, cultural and ancestral heritage. This mythology speaks of an age that existed long ago and yet remains in the present as a continuing, timeless experience linking past, present and future.

The Aborigines are natural conservationists. Their economy, based on the hunting activities of the men and the fishing and gathering of the women, was attuned to the regenerative capacity of the environment. For example, a good hunter who knew intimately the habits of his game and understood the changes of the seasons, took only what was needed to feed his people thereby keeping the balance with natural reproduction. Starvation was unknown in their fragile but complex land that would kill many white pioneers and settlers.

The Aborigines' relationship with the land was so intimate and complex that to uproot them from the land meant spiritual death. Alienation from the land meant alienation from Dreamtime.

Anthropologist W.E.H Stanner had this to say of the Aborigines-land relationship: "No English words are good enough to give a sense of the links between an Aboriginal group and its homeland. Our word 'home'... does not match the Aboriginal word that may mean 'camp', 'hearth', 'country', 'everlasting home', 'totem place', 'life source', 'spirit centre' and much else all in one ....When we took what we call 'land' we took what to them meant hearth, home, the source and locus of life, and everlastingness of spirit."

Modern Aborignal history is a long process of alienation of the Aborigines from the land. The narrative is complex, replete with moving stories of subjugation, compromise, resistance, revival and renewal and, ultimately, reunification with Dreamtime.

Without this perspective, it is difficult to understand the Aboriginal movement in Australia, and for that matter, the cause of the Maoris in Aotearoa (New Zealand), the South Pacific peoples and the indigenous peoples' movements elsewhere in the Asia-Pacific region.

Saviors of Agriculture

Peasant movements include organizations of farmers, fishers, indigenous peoples and rural women, and people's cooperatives, all generated and sustained endogenously or by urban-based institutions. The movements address a wide range of issues, including land tenure, inequalities in income and income distribution, public-policy biases against the rural sector, social-service delivery, trading and marketing, usury and deterioration of the environment.

The most potent peasant movements have been those associated with revolutionary projects, as in China and Indochina. In both failed and still-thriving revolutions — for example, in Indonesia, Thailand, Malaysia, the Philippines — peasant movements have been the base of national movements. Even in countries where national revolution is nowhere on the horizon, peasant movements still constitute the largest movements of the oppressed.

In the more industrialized countries like Japan and the newly industrializing countries (NICs) of South Korea and Taiwan, farmers' movements continue to be a significant although gradually diminishing force. Japan's 3 million farmers, represented by major farmers' federations linked to mainstream political parties, still greatly influence government policy formation.

In South Korea, the *Saemul Undong* or New Village Movement was created by the authoritarian elite to serve as its rural base for industrial take-off. In Taiwan, the Koumintang formed the Farmers' Associations, patterned after Mao's peasant movement, to link the government to the countryside. In both cases, the farmers' movements were the most powerful of the forces that shaped agricultural development.

In the Philippines, a major part of the peasant movement is communist-led and comprises the main rural base of the New People's Army. There are many independent peasant organizations which are influenced by other ideologies. Independent peasant organizing in the country has also been assisted by many rural-development NGOs. To counter both types of peasant movements, former President Marcos rapidly formed more than 20,000 farmers' cooperatives by using subsidized credit from the World Bank.

In South Asia, peasant movements and rural cooperativism are the single biggest force in the local economy and self-governance. South Asian NGOs, which are the largest in the world, are mostly rural development-oriented and benefit mainly peasants and the rural poor. Together, the peasant movements and the NGOs form the basis of grass-roots democracy.

Mass movements fighting for sustainable agriculture and rural development are emerging everywhere, inspired by the need to restore ecosystems degraded by years of colonial and modern agriculture and industrial exploitation. Sustainable-agriculture movements promote ecologically sound farming, land-tenure reform, food security, productivity comparable to that of chemical and modern agriculture, higher income and equitable income distribution, public services, calibrated industrialization, and science that does not violate nature.

Fishers' Organizations

Asia-Pacific claims millions of hectares of coastal and marine areas. Except for inhabitants of the interiors of China and South Asia and other land-locked countries, most Asians live near the coast. Fish and marine products and services are a major source of national revenue and household income; sea transport and tourism are also central to the economies of the region.

Fishers' organizations are organically linked to peasant movements because they also address agricultural problems. They are also linked to trade unionism by big commercial fishing, large-scale aquaculture and fishery-based industries. However, they are emerging as a distinct grass-roots movement. Fisherfolk have long fought for control over coastal and marine resources, and against overexploitative fishing giants, illegal fishing methods, industrial and human pollution, and the destruction of fish habitats.

Fishers' groups lead in advocating aquatic reform and in negotiating the law of the sea. Migratory fishstocks straddling territorial boundaries in the high seas, says the United Nations Conference on Environment and Development (UNCED), is also an outstanding issue.

Rediscovering the Roots

Ethnicity is a stranger to the traditional revolutionary paradigm, where indigenous peoples are no more than a mass of diminishing tribes to be won over lest they become enemies of the revolution. But now, indigenous peoples, oppressed by centuries of colonialism and marginalized by modernization, are central to the environment-versus-development debate.

Today the indigenous peoples are high on governments'and NGOs' list of priorities. Indigenous peoples are held to have the same rights as the enfranchised lowland citizens. They are the main protectors of the forests and upland ecosystems and other primary resources which are relentlessly overexploited by corporate interests. Their disappearing cultures seem to harbor the solution to the environment and development crisis confronting humanity.

Indigenous peoples from all around the world gathered at the Earth Summit in Rio de Janeiro in 1992 to claim their rightful place in the community of nations. *Agenda 21,* an environmental strategy produced by the Earth Summit, considers indigenous peoples as one of the nine major groups which will implement the global plan.

The United Nations declared 1993 as the International Year of the World's Indigenous Peoples, recognizing that these endangered *homo sapiens* are a major partner in development and saving the environment. The UN declaration spells out two aims: one is to strengthen international cooperation to solve problems of indigenous communities in education, human rights, the environment, development and health; another is to promote and encourage respect for human rights and freedom for all, irrespective of race, sex, language and religion.

Long before the UN, governments and multilateral development banks gave indigenous peoples their long-overdue recognition, environmentalists and peace activists had already done so as early as the 1960s. They were in the forefront of campaigns to monitor and stop nuclear testing and dumping of toxic and hazardous wastes in the South Pacific. Indigenous peoples rank high in Northern NGOs' list of priorities, and development projects intended for them are usually easily funded.

Indigenous peoples have a long tradition of asserting their right to self-determination and of resistance against domination. Beyond the issue of sovereignty is the question of sustainable development itself. It has dawned on the advocates of sustainable development that we need to re-examine our view of what makes an enduring society and that we must become ecocentric, as opposed to anthropocentric. Our new world view should include the key role of indigenous cultures and beliefs in social transformation.

The struggles for the rights of indigenous peoples strike at the heart of globalization from above, a process which concentrates resources and decisions in the hands of the major powers. The aboriginal movements in Australia, the Maori people's struggle in Aotearoa (New Zealand), the nuclear-free and independence movements in the South Pacific island-states, and the struggle for nationhood of the Kanaks and the East Timorese are all examples of movements for self-determination. Like the American Indians, indigenous peoples in Asia-Pacific have been pushed to near extinction by genocide, colonization, resettlement, population control and destruction of their homelands and cultures.

Through years of resistance, the indigenous peoples have preserved their tradition, culture, language, religion — their way of life — against relentless attempts to assimilate them and other oppressive policies of settlers and states. Their resistance teaches useful lessons in protecting diversity of cultures in face of homogenization and massive violation of human rights. In the mid-1970s, for example, the Cordillera peoples of northern Philippines showed how a united struggle could stop construction of a multimillion-dollar dam project funded by the World Bank.

Rethinking the Role of Trade Unions

Workers have always been a major force in modern history and in the most significant transformations in the Asia-Pacific region. *Agenda 21* cites them and trade unions as one of the nine groups with a major role in implementing the global plan.

Industrial workers are but a small fraction of the nearly 3 billion people in Asia, but wield power disproportionate to their number. They are the main builders of the industrial societies of Japan, Australia, and New Zealand. They helped to realize the economic miracles of the NICS. They are the principal modernizing sector of the emerging economies of the basically agrarian countries of the Asia-Pacific region.

The workers were the first to be enfranchised among the underclasses. Not only did they exercise the right of suffrage much ahead of the other oppressed and exploited classes, they have also made and unmade governments through their collective power and political parties. Their muscle has been flexed in Australia, New Zealand, Japan, India, China, Indochina and North Korea. But this is only half of the story. The other half is about how labor has become a major force of conservatism and a defender of an obsolete model of development.

For reasons that have been adequately articulated in a panoply of socialist, and even conservative, literature, the workers are the most inclined toward voluntary and collective action. They have a time-tested democratic institution, the trade union, through which they can participate in economic as well as political affairs.

Workers' movements, found in most Asian-Pacific countries, are the most highly organized and, as a rule, are a major part of social movements. In the traditional revolutionary model, they lead other mass movements. But they are also more subject than others to the influences of political parties and their state agenda. Their inclination toward self-governance stops at the factory premises. Outside the factory lies the world of politics and the struggle for state power. Here, trade unions tend to be adjuncts of political parties, whether in power or waiting for electoral victory.

Trade unions are generally internationalist in outlook. The inexorable movement of capital has linked every corner of the world to the world economic order. Workers' movements realize that they are organically linked to one another. Trade union movements in Asia are connected to various international organizations, the largest of which are the International Confederation of Free Trade Unions (ICFTU), the World Federation of Trade Unions (WFTU) and the World Congress of Labor (WCL), each wielding ideological influence, from conservatism to socialism.

A product of Western democratic tradition, trade unions came to Asia with colonialism. They emerged in the late 19th and early

20th centuries when Western democratic influences began to take root, mainly in the cities, mines, lumber camps and plantations.

Following the European socialist tradition, many Asian trade unions started as cooperative societies before plunging into the politics of collective bargaining, first at the factory and then at the industry level. Factory unions grew into federations and then into trade-union centers which linked Asian labor movements to each other and to global trade unions.

Internationalism and hierarchy in the labor movement grew from workers' realization that their enemy, capital, was boundless and veering toward monopoly. To win the battle against capital, the workers had to build structures traversing the boundaries of firms and nation states. Theoretically, workers are less interested in self-governance than the capture of state power as a strategy for emancipation.

Trade unions and workers' parties in the Asia-Pacific have always led movements for social and national change. They were at the vanguard of revolutions in China, North Korea, Vietnam, Laos and Cambodia. They forced regimes out of power in Japan, Australia, New Zealand and parts of India. Worker-based citizens' movements felled dictators in the Philippines, Bangladesh and Nepal. Even where less successful, they continue to be a hegemonic factor in social movements, challenging state and corporate systems.

The biggest resistance to the authoritarian elite of South Korea was initiated by workers, thousands of whom confronted the power structures beginning in 1987 and led the long drawn-out strike in the strategic Hyndai shipyard in April 1989. The middle class joined the struggle, forming a powerful national movement that toppled the Chun dictatorship.

But times are changing fast, more so since the collapse of socialism in Central Europe and the former Soviet Union. The historic changes have a far-reaching and profound impact on the role of workers and the trade-union movements in social and national transformation. Social movements are now thoroughly re-examining the revolutionary model that revered workers if they have not completely rejected it.

Three other trends might explain the dwindling influence of workers, trade unions and their political parties. One, key countries that still adhere to the socialist vision, like China and Vietnam, are rapidly turning from the state-dominated economy to the free-market system, necessarily undermining constitutionally guaranteed wages and benefits that workers have enjoyed for decades. The role and position of the workers and trade unions have been downgraded and subordinated to that of the emergent entrepreneurial class.

Two, many now see industrialism, which gave the workers their honored role, as responsible for many of the troubles confronting humanity. While the economic miracles of the NICs have not lost their allure for governments and big business, their viability and desirability are being questioned by citizens' movements.

Three, the regime changes and challenges to dominant paradigms have given birth to a new type of social movement that is no longer worker-dominated but cuts across social classes. In these emergent broad citizens' movements hegemony belongs to those who can challenge and offer alternatives to orthodoxies. Working-class vanguardism is out; dynamic plurality is in.

The Rise of Citizens' Movements

Civic responses to the endemic crisis of participation cross class boundaries. Traditional categories are proving inadequate for identifying "friends" and "enemies" who, many now realize, can come from any class or institution and may switch roles so unexpectedly that the fixed lines of old are blurred.

Although rooted in the earlier conventional mode of social mobilization, citizens' movements which rose in the 1970s and 1980s were multiclass or "supraclass" in membership and leadership.

Previous revolutions were also multiclass, but the mass of participants came mainly from peasants and workers, and leadership was usually assumed by workers' political parties. In contrast, the citizen uprisings in Iran in 1979, in the Philippines in 1986 and in South Korea in 1990, and the democratic upsurge in China in 1989 and

Guarding the Sacred Ballot

Whether under a democratic or authoritarian set-up, many politicians will not easily give up their tested weapons to seize power and keep it. In the Philippines, these weapons are called "three magic Gs" — goons, guns and gold. These politicians first try to buy votes and, failing in this, they resort to outright terror.

Post-WWII elections in many Asian countries have been marked not only by violence but also by heroic citizens' actions to guard the sanctity of the ballot. In the Philippines the tradition of citizens' movements for free elections goes back to the 1950s and earlier. The National Movement for Free Elections (NAMFREL) was the first national movement to mobilize thousands of volunteers around non-partisan activities, such as voters' education, campaigns for clean and fair elections, poll watching and ballot counting.

The tradition continues to this day as even more groups take part in protecting the ballot. The 1984 and 1986 elections called by former President Marcos saw tens of thousands of citizens risk their lives and limbs to ensure that voters could exercise their free choice and that every vote was counted. Those events are captured by photographic images of ordinary citizens on 24-hour vigils, and nuns, priests and high-society women in a tug-of-war with armed men and escorting ballot boxes to their destinations.

In Thailand, Burma, Kampuchea, South Korea, Nepal and other countries which have recently undergone transitions to democracy, citizens banded together into movements to press for new constitutions and free elections.

Seikatsu Club Cooperative Movement

Among the cooperative movements in Asia-Pacific, the Seikatsu Club Consumers' Cooperative (SCCC) in Japan is probably one of the biggest and most successful. By 1991 the SCCC had expanded to 12 prefectures, enlisted 200,000 member households or about 800,000 individuals, and was running an alternative domestic economy valued at 600 billion yen.

The SCCC was started in 1965 by a Tokyo housewife who initiated bulk buying to get cheaper milk. From this modest beginning the SCCC has grown into an economic giant distributing 400 products, all produced according to strict environmental and social standards, to 20,000 local groups of some eight-member-families each. The Club also uses its multimillion-dollar member-investment to produce its own goods when other producers do not meet the Club's set standards for product quality.

The Club's other activities include the formation of worker collectives to generate employment for its members, campaigns around human rights, peace and environmental issues, and participation in elections. In the May 1991 unified local election as many as 52 Seikatsu Club candidates won assembly seats.

In its struggle for social, political and economic reforms, the Seikatsu Club Cooperative Movement advocates what it calls citizens' *seikatsusha* social participation model. Held up as an alternative paradigm to capitalism and socialism, this model envisions a social system based on people's participation, cooperation, decentralization of authority and self-government.

the citizen revolutions in Eastern Europe and former Soviet Union which began in 1989, drew their mass support from the entire citizenry and a leadership not distinctly proletarian.

The struggles for participation are common to both the capitalist and socialist systems. Indeed, citizen responses are not particularly motivated by the ideological basis of either system but by the elite's monopoly of power. The endemic crisis of poverty and environment has closed the traditional ideological divide. Rights, development and environment have ceased to be class issues and are now issues for every citizen demanding a more equitable and sustainable society.

The encompassing issue of rights inspires citizens to voluntary action to expand their choices in life, to exercise self-determination, to fight for good government, to create an equitable and stable social order and a better quality of life.

Women at the Forefront

Peasants and workers continue to provide the base of voluntary movements, but women's emancipation movements have recently emerged as a more powerful force. They were the most effective lobbyists in UNCED before the Rio Earth Summit and the Global Forum in 1992. Women's movements are one of the nine major groups mandated by the UN to implement the Rio agreements.

Earlier, women's emancipation movements focused on suffrage rights. Later, Marxism influenced women's concerns to cover women's exploitation and oppression. Today, women's emancipation movements still bear the marks of liberalism and Marxism, but they now challenge the causes of the current environment and development crisis: not just class and social exploitation, but the male-dominated and male-oriented worldview of reality and development.

The strongest feminist organizations are found in Australia, India and the Philippines. Their numbers are difficult to ascertain, but their collective voice and influence penetrate all classes and sectors of society. There are women's organizations among the workers, peas-

Japanese Housewives in Environmental Activism

Mary Goebel Noguchi, assistant professor in the Law Department of Ritsumeikan University in Kyoto, wrote "The Rise of the Housewife Activist" (*Japan Quarterly*, July-September 1992), posing the following questions: "Imagine an environmental activist. Now look closely at the picture you have conjured up for yourself. What is the activist's sex? Age? Race? Educational and family background? Marital status?

"If you are an average American, a Robert Redford type may well have come to mind: young, white, middle-class, male — undoubtedly college-educated and most likely single. It may come as a surprise, then, to learn that in Japan the kind of person most apt to represent an environmental concern on a television program or in the printed media is a middle-aged woman who calls herself a housewife."

According to Jonathan Holliman in his article "Environmentalism with a Global Scope" in the 1990 *Japan Quarterly,* there are an estimated 3,000 active grass-roots conservation organizations throughout Japan. For example, a loose network of recycling groups formed the Japan Recycling Citizens' Center with about 40,000 supporters. Several consumers' organizations and consumers' cooperatives are also involved in a wide range of environmental issues.

The most striking feature of this array of small organizations, Noguchi says, "is that so many are run not out of offices by paid professionals but out of homes by volunteer housewives." The increasing participation of Japanese women, especially housewives, was also noted by *Japan Times* in 1991 in an article about groups that are in contact with the National Center for Citizens' Movements (NCCM), a Tokyo-based organization that monitors the activities of Japanese NGOs. The NCCM chief of staff, Suda Harumi, a male, confirmed the trend, saying that "almost all environmental groups are run by housewives."

Noguchi interviewed six of these housewives and came up with an interesting profile of the leadership of the grass-roots environmental movement. The six were highly educated mothers ranging from 37 to 70 years old. They became involved in environmental activism at different times, one of them as early as 1960.

A deeper inquiry into this contemporary trend in Japan reveals some interesting insights. One writer, Takie Sugiyama, asserts that "a professional housewife has some time to offer for volunteer work and that her responsibility for monitoring the family health may induce her to be alert to health hazards like industrial pollution, food poisoning, medical malpractices, which may involve her in consumer movements and ultimately in politics."

Another, Jonathan Holliman, suggests that Japanese men have defaulted on social involvement for some understandable reasons. He notes that "after commuting two or three hours a day and spending long hours at the office or factory most working people have little time or energy left to participate in community affairs. In this situation, it is mainly housewives who have both the free time and the concern for environmental health."

Whatever the reasons, and there are many, nobody can deny that Japanese women are breaking new ground in social activism. The political changes sweeping across Japan since the mid-1980s have seen the rise of such women political leaders as Takako Doi, the passage of the Equal Employment Opportunity Law, and the so-called "Madonna movement" in the late 1980s through which Japanese women voters helped deliver the ruling Liberal Democratic Party its first major electoral loss since 1955. These events, among other things, have given the Japanese women what Noguchi calls "a newfound sense of freedom and power, while making local governments more responsive to their demands."

With all these to boost their position in society, the Japanese women are definitely a growing force for change in Japan. The emergence of the housewife activist at the leadership of environmental movements adds more color to this phenomenon.

ants, indigenous people, in the urban poor communities, among consumers, in the so-called NGO community, in the academic and professional community, in government, in business, and among the middle class and the rich.

Cooperativism among poor women is strong. In South Asia, savings and credit organizations of peasant women are the best example of how the poor can mobilize resources and build and manage alternative systems for financing their own development projects. Indigenous women's groups are among the most outspoken critics of the model of development that they believe undermines their rights and destroys their fragile habitats.

Women are prominent in some Asian trade unions. In South Korea, for example, women workers, who comprise more than half the labor force, were in the forefront of thousands of strikes and street marches from 1987 to 1990. Organizations of women workers have also been formed in the Philippines and other countries.

Women are in the thick of other citizens' movements for consumerism, environmentalism, peace and security, population and health. Women's emancipation movements might even one day replace workers' parties as the vanguard and lead other social movements with a new perspective and vision of development.

The Young Stake their Claim

Youth and children are also gradually taking responsibility for the future of the region. In the UNCED Prepcom 4 in March-April 1992 in New York, youth leaders spoke for the young in a closing statement delivered before the final plenary session. In the hallowed halls of the UN they vented their disappointment with the older generation and staked their claim on and responsibility for the future.

There are thousands of associations of youth and children in the schools, workplaces, cities and villages. Most NGOs are run by people who were once involved in the youth and student movements.

Feared by elites and governments, youth movements have always added fire and spirit to mass movements and great social upheavals all over the world. Youth associations mobilized massively during the Vietnam war. More recently, they led the Tien An Men uprising. Idealism and dynamism — and, negatively, the prospect of an uncertain future — drive the youth to voluntary action.

Fusing Human Rights, Environment and Development

Environmentalism is a recent phenomenon. It began in the West with the peace movement of the 1960s which had strong ecological overtones, sparked mainly by the massive defoliation caused by US bombings of Indochina. Perhaps environmentalism lagged behind other causes because the ecological space of Asia-Pacific remains wide; its source and sink capacity have yet to be exhausted. Environmental issues were of marginal interest to social movements until the 1980s. Human rights and development were the focus of voluntary action from the 1960s to the 1980s, the decades of authoritarian development which saw many countries, led by South Korea and Taiwan, fall under dictatorships.

Human rights became central to social movements and were propelled mainly by the middle classes. In the 1980s, human-rights movements took on development and environmental concerns. The meeting of 202 Asian human-rights organizations in 1993, preparatory to the June UN World Conference on Human Rights in Geneva, attests not only to the comprehensive nature of human-rights advocacy but also to the strength of human-rights organizations in the region.

Environmentalism in Asia has been greatly influenced by Western ecological movements. The "hippie" generation of the 1960s inspired similar "back-to-nature" movements in Asia which drew many young people toward greater concern for environmental protection and traditional cultures and religion, especially Indian spiritualism.

Asian social movements linked environment and development only in the late 1980s. Earlier, citizen action on environmental issues was sporadic and isolated. There was little public awareness of the extent and potential threat of rainforest destruction, chemical agriculture, overfishing and industrial pollution until just before the UNCED meetings, after which environmentalism took giant strides forward.

Meanwhile, the consumers' movement has gained headway, especially in Malaysia, the Philippines and Japan. Where it once focused on prices and product quality, it has now taken up environmental safety and consumption patterns that stress ecosystems.

Since colonial times, Asia-Pacific has seen major conflicts among the global powers. Now citizen's movements against militarization and nuclear proliferation are part of the broad movement whose long-term goals are peace and security.

The Spiritual and Ethical Dimension

The citizens' movements which have brought about some of the most dramatic changes in 20th century Asia-Pacific are yet to be fully understood. Explanations from purely social, economic, political and cultural perspectives appear to be insufficient.

One missing link that has come into the discourse is the spiritual and ethical dimension of struggle. The issues around which thousands, nay millions, of citizens mobilize and risk their lives have a moral value. These citizens see their struggles as a moral cause, a fight between good and evil. Being on the side of the good gives people spiritual strength. This invisible inspiring element also serves to cement the solidarity among the actors.

The spiritual dimension is an integral part of the struggles of indigenous people and minorities in Asia-Pacific. They invoke the power of the spirits whenever they defend a tree against commercial loggers or a river against a dam project. This holds true for the Australian aborigines, the Maoris of New Zealand, the Polynesians and all indigenous peoples and tribes in Asia-Pacific.

The influence of Islam, Hinduism, Buddhism, Christianity and other religions also runs deep. It affects rulers and ruled alike. Religions and their can be a stabilizing or destabilizing force. Their in-

Human Chain and the Churches in South Korea

On 15 August 1993, 60,000 men and women linked arms to form a 50-kilometer-long human chain in South Korea to symbolize their long-standing desire for reunification of their divided country. The human chain started from the Independence Park in Seoul and went up to the dividing line at Panmunjom.

The human chain is a modern form of *Kang-kang-su-wul-le* which is derived from a traditional Korean play where women held hands forming a circle, singing, dancing and wishing upon the moon. It has been adopted by peace and environmental movements in other parts of the world.

The August 1993 mobilization, also called the South-North Human Chain for Peace and Reunification Rally, was initiated and organized by the Korean churches. A total of 49 denominations are involved in the reunification movement led by the National Council of Churches of Korea (NCCK) which itself has only six member churches.

The Allied Forces divided the Korean peninsula in 1945, separating 10 million families at the 38th parallel which split the country into the communist North and the anti-communist South. Since then, reunification has been a running theme in the activities of various citizens' groups and the churches in South Korea. Although muffled for a long time, the aspiration for reunification has resonated in recent years following the successes of citizens' mobilizations against the authoritarian order.

Many Korean churches have consistently supported people-empowerment activities, ranging from organizing trade unions and campaigns for democratic constitution and elections to environmental protection and national reunification.

❧

tervention or non-intervention makes and unmakes political regimes or, at the very least, influences social changes.

The Iranian people's revolution that overthrew the Shah in 1979 is an outstanding example of the power of religion. Islamic values inspired the revolution from its beginning until the climactic fall of the government and after.

In the Philippines, the citizens' revolution that toppled the Marcos regime drew support from the churches, both spiritually and materially. Church-inspired social action has long been part of the social movement in the country; words of support from church heirarchies even lent legitimacy to extra-legal initiatives of the citizens.

In South Korea, the citizens' movements would not have been as successful without the support of the Christian churches. The Chun government came under pressure not just from the workers, students and middle classes, but also from the local churches which were, in turn, supported by international organizations such as the World Council of Churches.

In other parts of Asia-Pacific, citizen mobilizations are influenced by values formed under one or other type of religious inspiration.

Information Flow

Democratization of information is a big factor in the growth and success of citizens' movements. Although the ownership and modes of utilization of information continue to be monopolized by a few, modern communications technologies have made information more accessible to a great number of people.

Grass-roots organizations and NGOs in Asia-Pacific relate to each other face to face and indirectly through a variety of communications media. Telephones, faxes, modems, VCRs, radios and printed media complement and sometimes substitute for direct communication among themselves.

Suppression of information always accompanies authoritarian regimes. Yet even under the strictest of conditions, citizens are able to find ways to get the information flowing. The authorities themselves, whose legitimacy is under question, help create the forces that one day will topple them. They have to provide better education to produce a highly educated work force needed for economic take-off. In the process, they produce educated citizens who demand more freedoms.

This is the irony vividly illustrated in the case of the Asian "economic miracles." In South Korea and Taiwan, for example, the citizens' movements that challenged authoritarian governments saw the participation of highly educated citizens.

The value and impact of the media may be difficult to determine. But it is safe to say that television, radio, newspapers and other forms of media have been important in shaping mass behavior and in deciding the outcomes of dramatic social changes in Asia-Pacific. Certainly, media played a role in galvanizing people's responses, in deterring dictators from engaging in mass slaughters in the Philippines, South Korea, Nepal, Bangladesh, Thailand and elswhere, and even just letting people know what is happening in a far-flung forest.

The extensive local, regional and international networks of NGOs and people's organizations serve as channels for information flow. These networks will continue to be crucial not only in spreading knowledge but also in strengthening solidarity across national borders.

CHAPTER 5

LOCAL DEVELOPMENT AND SELF-GOVERNANCE

Democracy from below has two key elements: one is voluntary action and organized participation of citizens; the other is community-centeredness and horizontal spread of popular centers of power.

Voluntary action involving masses of people democratizes society. The more inclusive the participation, the more democratic the outcome. The spread of decision-making power across sectors countervails the monopoly of power by government and corporations.

However, plurality in decision-making does not necessarily lead to local development and self-governance. Social movements, especially workers' and trade union movements and trade union-influenced sectoral movements, for example, have followed a vertical path of organization.

Local development and self-governance require deliberate re-orientation of voluntary action. Creating a favorable national climate is essential to expand the space for local initiatives. But for democratization to be thoroughgoing, decision-making has to be pulled down to the lowest possible level at which small groups and even individuals can exercise control.

Democratization at the subnational level is happening not only in isolated communities; NGO-supported grass-roots movements are working everywhere to transform local communities and their environments through a holistic area development strategy.

Area Development

The concept of integrated area development has evolved over time. In the 1970s, it was promoted by bilateral and multilateral agencies such as the United States Agency for International Development (USAID) and the World Bank. The integrated area development strategy required concentration of development assistance in areas such as agricultural basins to build a geophysical framework for local government development efforts directed by a central authority.

Integrated area development failed to break the sectoral orientation of line agencies or effect any real decentralization of state-led development. Allocation of resources continued to be dictated from above and power never trickled down to the grass-roots. Intra-government dynamics and corruption and lack of popular involvement doomed the project to failure. Save for some new infrastructure, local areas remained as they were before the project.

However, there is another kind of integrated area development which is rooted in the revolutionary tradition. Mao's people's-war strategy, for example, required base-area building, or turning the backward regions of China into bastions of political and economic power from which the agrarian revolution was to be launched and the cities encircled. Mao realized his dream.

The concept of area as integrated system may be traced to the indigenous peoples. Because they will probably die where they were born, the indigenous peoples view their lives, the land, rivers, flora and fauna as one system. For them, the ecosystem is not just an idea but the reality of life itself.

People striving for integrated area development have learned, consciously or not, from the past. Despite their cultural differences, they share a common perspective and vision. Their efforts begin in the local community and their long-term goal is a better life, which includes a healthy environment.

Integrated area development varies from country to country. Where the ecosystem is the defining factor in development, as it is in

A Convergence for Area Development

The challenge to make an impact on the local economy and micro ecosystems has been taken up by many NGOs and grass-roots organizations across Asia-Pacific. The Convergence for Community-Centered Area Development (CONVERGENCE) in the Philippines is a network founded precisely for this purpose.

CONVERGENCE was formed in 1990 by about 20 Philippine NGOs with many years of experience in organizing local communities. These groups believed that by pooling their capacities and resources they could heighten their impact and bring about local transformation even without immediate dramatic changes at the macro level.

The group defined a scale of impact and sustainability according to socio-political, economic and ecological factors. An area usually consists of a small district or province of more than 1,000 square kilometers with around 400,000 inhabitants whose everyday life is woven around a local economic system linked to a major natural-resource base such as, for example, an agricultural basin or a fishing bay area.

By 1993, members of CONVERGENCE had experimented in area development in the uplands, lowlands and coastal ecosystems throughout the archipelago. Results are measured by increased local capacities in resource access and mobilization, poverty alleviation and sustainable livelihoods, and restoration of damaged micro ecosystems.

The positive results at the area level are solid inputs for policy advocacy at the higher level.

The Ting Hsien Experiment

It all began when a citizen responded to a basic human condition — illiteracy. The response became a lifetime commitment which in turn gave birth to a worldwide movement.

This, in brief, is the grand narrative of the rural reconstruction movement. The architect and creator was a Chinese scholar by the name of Dr. Y.C. James Yen, awarded in 1943 the Copernicus Citations as one of the 10 outstanding "modern revolutionaries" along with Albert Einstein, John Dewey, Walt Disney, Henry Ford, Orville Wright and others.

In the battlefields of France during WWI, Dr. Yen, then a YMCA volunteer, worked as interpreter for the 200,000 Chinese coolies who were sent by China to dig trenches and build roads for the Allied Forces. One day a coolie requested Dr. Yen to write a letter to his family. The next day Dr. Yen had a pile of similar requests. He then decided to teach the coolies to read and write and soon realized the enormous potential power he had unlocked among his downtrodden countrymen. It was a classic validation of the adage, "Give man a fish and he lives for a day; teach him to fish and he lives for a lifetime."

The experience was a turning point for Dr. Yen. It inspired him to dream of peasant emancipation through a mass education movement. Further analysis brought Dr. Yen to a definition of the rural problematique as the interlocking of ignorance, poverty, disease and civic inertia. The solution, he argued, could only be an integrated one, a dynamic interplay of education, livelihood, health and self-governance. Thus was born the rural reconstruction movement and the so-called four-fold approach to peasant emancipation.

In the late 1920s, Dr. Yen began his experiment in Northern China in a district called Ting Hsien. In this county of 480 square miles, 472 villages and about 400,000 inhabitants, he tested his vision of rural reconstruction which he alternately called human reconstruction.

The experiment began with a literacy program. It utilized the "People's Thousand Character Texts" prepared by Dr. Yen himself on the basis of the spoken language of the people. The module could be mastered by the average illiterate in four months, working only an hour a day. A complete system of education evolved, covering organization, teacher training and supervision. The emphasis later shifted from extensive promotion of literacy to intensive study of life in the rural districts. All this took the character of a massive movement.

The Ting Hsien project was complemented by mobilization of citizens from the upper and middle classes. A leading Peking daily reported at that time: "It was the most magnificent exodus of the intelligentsia into the country that has taken place in Chinese history to date. Holders of old imperial degrees, professors of national universities, a college president and former member of the National Assembly, and a number of PhDs and MDs from leading American universities left their positions and comfortable homes in the cities to go to the backwoods of Ting Hsien, to find ways and means to revitalize the life of an ancient, backward people, and to build democracy from the bottom up."

The mobilization was aided by a simple set of slogans:

Go to the people.

Live among them.

Learn from them.

Love them.

Serve them.

Plan with them.

Start with what they know.

Build on what they have.

These were reminiscent of Confucian one-liners which Mao himself adopted in his own revolution. They seemed so simple and yet so rich in values that guided the thousands of enlightened citizen volunteers who were motivated to come down "from the ivory tower to the mudhouse."

Education for self-governance was the central theme of Yen's project. He said, "What good is it to fatten a man's purse, teach him to read and write, and help him toward better health, if he remains dependent on government and others? He must be taught the responsibility of citizenship in a democratic society, shown how to band with his neighbors to run community affairs. Education in citizenship is at the very core of rural reconstruction. Self-government is not a gift from above; it's an achievement by the people."

The Ting Hsien experiment was replicated in many parts of China. The results, matched or surpassed only by Mao's revolution, were amazing. Pearl S. Buck, 1938 Nobel Prize winner in literature, had this to say of Dr. Yen and his movement: "He taught many millions of his countrymen to read and established hundreds of rural centers to combat poverty and disease, to reform land tenure and to develop self-government. What he accomplished history will record as one of the great constructive achievements of our time."

Rural reconstruction movement in China spread to other parts of the world after WWII. The first to follow after the China experience was the Philippine Rural Reconstruction Movement begun in 1952 with active participation by Dr. Yen himself. In the course of seven decades beginning from the 1920s, the rural reconstruction movement has gained foothold in the continents of Asia, Latin America and Africa.

the upland indigenous communities or lowland agricultural basins, the area is designed around the watershed. Where geopolitics is the prime consideration, the area follows political boundaries.

Area scope likewise varies greatly, depending on geophysical, demographic, political and economic factors and, most important, scale of an area. In some countries, areas are only as big as a district or province. In others, they are no less than a bioregion spanning several districts or provinces, such as the desert of Rajasthan in India.

The scale of an area is derived from the requirements of local development and self-governance, and starting baselines and desired ends, as defined by the local communities and people's organizations themselves. The answers to the following questions will determine scale. Is the area large enough to permit local autonomous development? What is the state of its resources? What is the impact of external factors on resources? What is a manageable size for building the local economy? What size of population will allow the people to govern themselves?

The area-development framework does not only define the physical and demographic parameters of local development and self-governance; it is also the basis for addressing development and environment issues and for designing programs and projects. Development can be carried out and sustained in this micro framework.

Translation into action of big plans such as *Agenda 21* cannot remain at the national level. It has to be carried out at the subnational level as well. The area-development framework will be a major crucible for testing them. All UNCED agreements, plans, programs and corporate activities have to find their place in the local communities and the local ecosystems.

The area-development framework eases the monitoring of the implementation of sustainable development plans. The results at the local level will tell us whether there are advances in democratization and development, restoring biodiversity and the process of slowing down atmospheric emissions.

Area development is ultimately a struggle for local sovereignty. It is a direct counterpoint to the national and international monopoly of resources and decision-making power. Colonization and modernization have sapped the life resources of local communities through extractive industries, trade and taxation. Local communities are dumping sites of surplus products and the wastes of the rich nations. As a result, local communities have little control over their own life and development.

A sustainable area-development process hinges on the regaining of sovereignty by local communities which must dictate the substance and direction of their own development and end the net resource outflow. Thousands of grass-roots and development support organizations are striving to regain their sovereignty by promoting integrated area development. Their activities include awareness raising, organization and leadership building, land and asset reform, management training, natural-resources management, livelihood-systems development, savings and credit and alternative development financing, sustainable agriculture, micro enterprises, alternative trading and marketing, and improving service-delivery systems.

Through consciousness-raising programs local communities become aware of their own realities as well as of greater society's, of the development-versus-environment debate and of the imperative of voluntary action. NGOs help local communities acquire skills in scale management and organization. Primary people's institutions, such as sectoral associations, cooperatives and community organizations, eventually grow into area-level structures of self-governance. They also launch local and national campaigns against poverty and for welfare, reform and environmental protection.

These local communities engage in livelihood activities designed to build a community-centered economy attuned to the carrying capacity of the environment and based on sustainable agriculture and rural development. Alternative financial systems, from micro savings and credit schemes to people's banks, mobilize the funds. Alternative trading and marketing reduce and eventually eliminate the exploitative monopoly traders and directly link rural producers to urban consumers. The more successful communities now trade globally.

A new experiment, the local exchange and trading system in Australia and other countries, seeks to cut the local economy off from the global system by localizing currencies. Patterned after Robert Owen's labor exchange in England in the 19th century and similar efforts in Austria, the US and Canada, the system is successful only in small areas. Whether it will work elsewhere on a larger scale remains to be seen.

Restoring damaged ecosystems is a tall order. Activities and funding for environmental protection, restoration and management have increased visibly. Local communities and NGOs are mobilizing massively for conservation and development of the integrated protected areas systems, community-based agroforestry, watershed protection and management, and coastal and marine-resources management.

The most popular campaigns to save the forests have been mounted by the indigenous peoples and local communities in Sarawak, Thailand, Indonesia, the Philippines and India. These campaigns target governments, the multilateral development banks and the timber companies.

Despite significant advances in environmental protection, controversies remain: the subordination of indigenous peoples and local communities to external profit-seeking groups in the conservation and management of the forests; persistent logging, inadequate state policies and laws; poor enforcement of laws; intervention by foreign NGOs; and funding by the World Bank and the Asian Development Bank of projects that undermine conservation, such as the construction of big dams in forests. High consumption in rich countries such as Japan also sets back environmental protection because it is one of the causes of poverty and misery in the less-developed countries.

Local communities and NGOs draw local authorities, one of the groups that will carry out *Agenda 21*, into efforts to promote local development and self-governance. Although some government policies and projects using public resources have improved the lives of the local people and protect the ecosystems, it remains to be seen how far local authorities can translate *Agenda 21* into action.

Official development assistance for area development is sorely inadequate. Not only does it fail to reverse the net outflow of resources from communities, but it has been used to promote globalization that undermines local autonomous development.

In contrast, donor NGOs in the North, such as NOVIB (Netherlands), support local efforts at integrated area development in different parts of Asia although the impact of funds and other forms of assistance on local self-reliance is yet to be fully evaluated.

The people-to-people aid movement formed in 1989 in Japan strives to mobilize citizens and resources to help its counterpart people's movements in Asia. It also strengthens citizen-to-citizen links through exchange programs and lobbies against government policies and Japanese corporations which harm Asian communities.

Village Institutions in India

By Anil Agarwal and Sunita Narain
Centre for Science and Environment

Government programmes have over the years created a feeling of total dependence within the people. Today, villagers not only expect the government to build roads and schools and give them employment but also plant trees and grasses and look after their local water sources like ponds and tanks.

This has been self-defeating. The natural resource base of a village can only be managed by the villagers themselves. Rational use and maintenance of village land and water resources needs discipline. Villagers have to ensure that animals do not graze in their protected commons, the catchments of their local water bodies are conserved and properly used, and the common produce from these lands is equitably distributed within the village. The government cannot do this in each and every village of India. Environmental regeneration in every village of India is a task that the people must undertake themselves.

The villagers can do all this and more, only if there is an effective village-level institution to energise and involve them in controlling and managing their environment, and to resolve any disputes that may arise amongst them. Unfortunately, there is no effective forum in Indian villages today for this purpose.

Voluntary agencies are often cited as effective agents for ensuring people's participation in rural development programmes. We have found that all good cases of environmental regeneration undertaken by voluntary agencies are invariably those cases where voluntary agencies have set up an effective institution at the village level. In all these cases, the role of the voluntary agency has largely been to create an effective village-level institution and then give moral, technical and financial support to it. But it is the creation of a village-level institution which brings the people together, spurs them into action and ensures the protection and the development of the natural resource base.

The Village of Sukhomajri

The village of Sukhomajri near Chandigarh, has been widely hailed for its pioneering efforts in microwatershed development. The inhabitants of Sukhomajri have protected the heavily degraded forest land that lies within the catchment of their minor irrigation tank. The tank has helped to increase their crop production nearly three times and the protection of the forest area has greatly increased grass and fodder availability. This in turn has greatly increased milk production. In just about five years, annual household incomes have increased by an estimated Rs.2000 to 3,000 — a stupendous achievement by any count and all of it has been achieved through the improvement of the village natural resource base and self-reliance. Few government schemes can boast of such results.

The crucial role in this entire exercise was played by a village-level institution that was specifically created in Sukhomajri for the purpose. This institution called the Hill Resources Management Society, consists of one member from each household in the village. Its job is to provide a forum for the villagers to discuss their problems, mobilise them to take control over their environment and ensure discipline amongst its members. The society makes sure that no household grazes its animals in the watershed and in return it has created a framework for a fair distribution of the resources so generated — namely, water, wood and grass — amongst all the households in the village. Today the entire catchment of the tank is green and the village is prosperous, capable of withstanding drought.

The Chipko Movement

Nowhere in the world has a more successful community afforestation programme been organised than the one spearheaded by the Chipko Movement under the leadership of the Dasholi Gram Swarajya Mandal in Gopeshwar. The Mandal has organised an informal village-level institution in each of the villages it is working. This institution — a Mahila Mangal Dal — consists of a woman member from each household in the village. These village dals have slowly taken control of the community lands surrounding their villages. They protect these lands, plant trees on them and ensure fair distribution of the grass and fodder that becomes available in increased quantities from these lands. The forum of the Mahila Mangal Dal provides the women of these villages an opportunity to get together, discuss their problems, seek their solutions and assert their priorities. And now from afforestation, they are steadily moving towards articulating other needs and activities like provision of drinking water, schools for their children and primary health care facilities.

Pani Panchayats

The concept of Pani Panchayats, another type of village-level institution, was developed by Gram Gaurav Pratisthan in Pune to bring about equitable distribution of a scarce resource like water in an acutely drought prone area. This is an extremely difficult objective to achieve. Yet Pani Panchayats have done it.

They help villagers to discuss their problems and organise them to distribute irrigation water equitably. A Pani Panchayat consists of all marginal farmers, landless labourers and Harijans in a village — all of whom unite because of their common desire for irrigation water for their parched fields. Once water is made available, the panchayat controls its distribution, use and even the cropping pattern. For instance, all villages with Pani Panchayats have decided that water consuming crops like sugarcane will not be grown by their members so that the maximum number of members and the maximum amount of land can benefit from the limited water resources available.

Vankar Cooperatives

The St. Xavier's Behavioural Science Centre in Ahmedabad has been organising afforestation programmes in the highly saline lands of the Bhal area of Gujarat. The Centre has formed cooperatives in each of the villages it is working. The cooperatives consist of all households of the scheduled caste community of Vankars living in these villages. The cooperatives have undertaken afforestation projects on the community lands of Vankars. it seems that the state government had set up cooperatives of scheduled caste communities in the 1950s and had allotted land to them, but the land has since been lying waste. As the afforestation programme supported by the Behavioural Science Centre began to yield money — *Prosopis juliflora* trees were grown and their wood converted into charcoal — resentment within the dominant Rajput community also began to grow. But the cooperatives were able to continue their work and organise the poor Vankars to manage their community lands, earn money and achieve a high degree of economic independence.

The Village of Brahmano ka Verda

The panchayat of Brahmano ka Verda, a small village in the Aravalli Hills near Udaipur, also created numerous obstacles in the way of tribal women who wanted to take up an afforestation programme. Brahmano ka Verda is inhabited by both Brahmins and tribals who live in two separate hamlets. A voluntary agency called Sewa Mandir organised the tribal women to start income generating activities including afforestation of the common lands. The tribal women formed a cooperative to undertake an afforestation programme and asked the government to allot land. But their attempts were foiled for over four long years as the panchayat used every trick to stall its work. Under the prevailing land laws in the state, revenue land can be allotted to a cooperative but only after a formal committee set up by the sub-divisional magistrate has seen the site and approved the transfer. This seemingly simple process became a long battle. For almost four years, the allotment could not be made because the panchayat leaders would ensure that whenever the committee met, its quorum was incomplete. At one meeting the quorum was complete, but the patwari argued that this land was panchayat land and could not be transferred, contrary to the information that he himself had given the women's cooperative a few years ago that this was revenue land. The voluntary agency then helped the women to find the actual maps and take them back to the committee for approval. The entire matter took four years and only after enormous persistence the land was formally allotted. The cooperative faced this problem only because the panchayat, dominated by the Brahmins of the main settlement, did not approve of tribal women getting this land.

In Sukhomajri, the villagers argue that they could not have achieved what they have achieved if they had used the panchayat as their forum. They claimed that the panchayat leaders, who live in a neighbouring settlement, have no interest in the regeneration of their watershed. Moreover, the panchayat covers three to four villages and it never gets involved with the specifics of development in an individual village. It is for this reason that a separate society — the Hill Resource Management Society — had to be created exclusively for the villagers of Sukhomajri.

Bemru Gram Panchayat

The problems posed by involving panchayats in natural resource management can be further appreciated by taking a look at what is happening in the Bemru gram panchayat in the High Himalaya near Joshimath. The gram panchayat covers three villages but eight settlements in reality. The boundary of village Bemru covers a relatively large area of common land. This land has been traditionally used by some of the neighbouring settlements for their basic needs of fuel and fodder. This practice has been contiuing for decades. But during the recent panchayat elections, the villagers of Bemru told the villagers from the neighbouring settlements that they must support their candidate or else they will not let them graze their animals in their common lands or collect firewood. THe candidate of Bemru lost and in retaliation, Bemru's villagers stopped the use of their village commons by neighbouring villagers. This has lead to clashes and fights. The panchayat has become the cause of increased tensions over the use of the commons rather than a forum for resolving them.

The Village of Nada

Yet another example of the problems created by panchayats covering several settlements is provided by Nada, a small village near Chandigarh, where the Sukhomajri model of watershed development has been attempted. The village consists of four different hamlets, of which three are dominated by the relatively more powerful Rajput community and the third is exclusively inhabited by the Scheduled Castes and is called Harijan Nada. Separate dams have been built to store water for each hamlet. In fact, the implementing agency, recognising the inherent power of the Rajputs over the Harijans, built the height of one of the dams in such a way that water would reach only Harijan Nada which is situated at a lower level. This made it impossible for the Rajput hamlet to draw water from the dam meant to benefit Harijan Nada.

But another problem still remained. The people living in Harijan Nada have little land and require additional sources of income. The hamlet has formed a Hill Resources Management Society. It has protected the panchayat and forest land adjoining the hamlet and has taken the trouble to graze its animals further away. The hamlet now gets increased fodder as well as bhabbar grass — a raw material for rope making — which has increased their incomes. But the people in the Rajput hamlets also covet this produce, and being part of one panchayat, they insist that the grasses and trees now growing on the common land next to Harijan Nada belong to them also, though they have done nothing to protect or improve the land. Over the last few years, women from the Rajput hamlets have forcibly entered the protected area and cut the grass and trees. The people in Harijan Nada are helpless as the panchayat is common and the Rajputs have equal rights over the land. But they obviously resent it and if this goes on, they will stop protecting the area.

In several cases, we have found that the panchayats have actually got into direct conflict with the new village-level institutions created by the voluntary agencies. For instance, the Mahila Mangal Dals organised by the Chipko Movement have had constant conflicts with panchayat leaders, who have rarely shown interest in the development of village natural resources. They create obstacles for the Mahila Mangal Dals, especially when they try to improve panchayat lands. Being panchayat lands, the panchayat leaders try to assert their diktat which the women resent as it is they who do all the work to protect and improve the land.

Advocacy for Policy Reforms

Because local development and self-governance need a support-ive national policy, grass-roots movements and NGOs lobby to in-fluence public policy. Advocacy themes vary from country to coun-try. The concerns of citizens' movements in the rich countries, such as Japan, Australia, New Zealand and the NICs, differ from those in the poor countries, such as Bangladesh. Issues also differ from rich country to rich country. For example, those in Japan, a major global power, differ from those in Australia or New Zealand.

Similary, issues also differ among poor countries. China, for example, confronts problems different from those of India. A sur-vey of other poor Asian countries will no doubt yield a varied list of woes and priorities. But no matter how different the countries, they have much in common. Every issue they address is linked to the environment-versus-development debate, to disparities in and among countries, and to the right of citizens to demand public ac-countability and respect for human rights.

Equity is the most prominent of policy-advocacy themes. Cen-tral to sustainable development, the resolution of inequality between and within nations, between men and women, and between the present and future generations, will remove the main stumbling block that divides societies.

Two out of 10 Asians comprise the elite. Nationality matters little. Twenty percent of the population earns a per capita annual income of over US$20,000 and produces over 20,000 kilograms of waste per person yearly.

In contrast, five to seven of 10 Asians, depending on their coun-try, are poor and powerless. They live on US$2 dollars a day at most. They probably produce less than the 1,500 kilograms of waste per person annually, the global norm UN scientists say will enable hu-manity to sustain itself through to the 21st century, assuming con-stant population and no deforestation.

One can easily imagine the huge difference between the quality of life of the few and that of the vast majority. If this situation persists, there is no guarantee that Asia-Pacific will attain peace and security.

The idea that growth must be achieved at any cost prevails in the minds of most Asian leaders, whether in government or the corporate world, and is another focus of policy advocacy by citizens' movements. The fascination for growth is dangerous because it avoids the issue of equity. If all poor Asian countries grow like Japan and the NICs, future generations can kiss their future goodbye. To paraphrase Gandhi, India would never become another Great Britain because Great Britain was created at the expense of India and other countries like India.

Progressive citizens are aware of the dangers of ignoring equity for the sake of growth. Land reform, as part of asset reform, is a popular cause in the poor as well as middle-income countries of Asia because the skewed ownership structure of land symbolizes the great disparities in resource and power distribution. Citizens' movements also address problems of foreign debt, trade and investment, and aid, seeking debt relief, fairer trade terms and reversal of resource flows.

Citizens' movements work for the basic right of every citizen to demand good and responsive governance, inclusive participation and equal electoral opportunities. Citizens' electoral movements have a long tradition in countries such as the Philippines. In countries under authoritarian rule, such as Cambodia, these movements have created and expanded the scope of people's political participation.

Policy advocacy and area development are complementary dimensions of a holistic strategy for transforming the substance and process of development. Policy advocacy creates the climate for expanding area development and area development shapes policy advocacy.

Lack of appreciation of this dynamic creates tension within the voluntary sector. Some view policy advocacy, at the national and global levels, as work that achieves too little for the time and energy it requires. They sometimes deride it as elitist, largely dependent on a handful of "policy experts" and the globetrotting development

ADB NGO Lobby

As a major development institution, the Asian Development Bank (ADB) has become a focus of lobby activities of a growing number of NGOs and people's organizations within and outside the Asia-Pacific region. Since its founding in 1966, the ADB has financed development investments in its developing member countries (DMCs) amounting to $43 billion for a total of 1,180 projects in agriculture and agro-industry, energy, industry, transport and communications, social infrastructure, finance and the private sector. Its annual lending increased from $1.7 billion in 1981 to $5.3 billion in 1993.

The ADB NGO lobby began in 1989 through the initiative of two US NGOs — Friends of the Earth (FoE) and Environmental Policy Institute (EPI) — and the Asian NGO Coalition (ANGOC). All three have also been involved in the World Bank NGO lobby network. Since then, there has been a dramatic increase in the number of lobby groups demanding reforms in the policies and activities of the Bank.

The 25th ADB Annual Meeting in May 1992 in Hong Kong saw a significant expansion of the lobby network with the participation of the South-North Project for Sustainable Development in Asia (S-N Project). The S-N Project was a network organized in 1990 to do research and lobbying around the themes of agriculture, forestry and micro ecosystems. It was originally composed of six Asian organizations: AWARE (India); Project for Ecological Recovery (Thailand); PRRM (Philippines); PROSHIKA (Bangladesh); SAM (Malaysia); WALHI (Indonesia); and a donor-partner in the North, NOVIB (Netherlands). During the lobby phase, two more groups were enlisted into the network — Japan Tropical Forest Action Network (JATAN) and Bank Information Center-USA (BICUSA) — because of their track record in lobby work with multilateral development banks.

Participation in the lobby campaigns increased from 25 to over 30 organizations between the 25th (1992,Hong Kong) and 26th (1993, Manila) ADB annual meetings. Aside from members of the major networks, these included AID Watch (Australia), Greenpeace International, Sustainable Agriculture Network (SAN), Philippine Development Forum (US), Freedom from Debt Coalition (Philippines), Environmental Defense Fund (US) , Thailand Rural Reconstruction Movement (TRRM), among several others.

The NGO lobby has raised a variety of issues and concerns over the social and environmental impacts of Bank policies and projects. These issues have been forcefully backed up by case studies conducted by the NGOs in partnership with affected local communities.

ADB has been responding positively to NGO pressure for changes. Apart from liberal use of trendy sustainable-development rhetoric, ADB has recently issued new guidelines incorporating environment and social dimensions in policy formation and program and project cycles. ADB has also opened some space for NGO and local community participation in project implementation, monitoring and evaluation.

However, these reforms are considered by NGOs and local communities as too little and too slow in coming. A budget analysis reveals that the bulk of ADB's money still goes to traditional growth projects that produce adverse social and ecological effects. Justifiably so, the lobbyists continue to doubt if ADB is capable of making a fundamental shift in its strategic orientation, policies and activities.

🖉

The Poor Go Banking

Who says that the poor are not bankable? The truth is, the poor, indeed the poorest among them, have demonstrated often and in many parts of Asia that they can set up, own and run their own people's banks to finance their livelihood projects and other activities.

The most outstanding example so far is the world-reknowned Grameen Bank in Bangladesh. It is one of the most successful experiments in extending credit to the landless poor.

The Grameen Bank was conceived and developed by Professor Muhammad Yunus of Chittagong University in Bangladesh. It started in 1976 as an action-research project in the pilot village of Jobra. The first beneficiaries were the poor women weavers who were being exploited by moneylenders. Professor Yunus initially guaranteed bank loans to these poor women who had no collateral. This first try proved successful as indicated by above 99 percent repayment rates.

The Grameen Bank project struggled through many years to be what it is now — a bank largely owned by the poor for the poor. Seventy-five percent of the shares are owned by the landless borrowers and the rest by the Bangladesh government. As of 1992, Grameen Bank had more than 400,000 borrowers, and 82 percent of them were women. It lends out $2.5 million every month in tiny loans averaging $67, with a high recovery rate of 98 percent. Borrowers have accumulated a savings fund to the tune of $7 million, out of the negligible one taka per week required savings for each borrower.

The Grameen Bank Project (GBP) became a full-fledged bank in 1983. The Bangladesh government shouldered 60 percent of the initial paid-up capital with the borrowers providing the rest out of their savings. Foreign subsidy has been considerable but dependence on this has declined from 83 percent to 60 percent.

By 1991, the Grameen Bank's services had reached 23,000 of the 68,000 villages of Bangladesh through its more than 800 local branches. Some 1 million households have received credit. Intended principally for working capital, the loans have generated a great deal of employment, especially for rural women.

Grameen Bank is an innovative concept turned into reality. The elements of this successful innovation are organization, close relationship between bank and borrowers, deliberate intention to reach the poorest and the unhurried process of group formation itself. People are organized into groups of five and each member of the group has to guarantee the repayment of a loan to any of the other four members. The process is allowed to take its time, often expressed in these terms: "Why hurry? If poor people have survived without Grameen for all these years now, they will survive without it for some more years to come."

This deliberate phasing tells enough that development processes are complex and take time to produce certain outcomes, intended or not.

In many parts of Asia-Pacific many groups have been striving to set up their own alternative schemes to finance their economic activities. They have recognized they need a people's bank to build the local economy and redirect local development toward a more self-reliant path.

set. True enough, policy advocacy that is not well rooted in local community-based initiatives lacks substance and will most likely run out of steam in the long haul.

But to reduce everything to local empowerment and community development is one type of fundamentalism; it may be called "area determinism" or "ecoanarchism". It can foster the illusion that area development can be sealed off from external influences and mature entirely on its own.

Local areas are the ultimate site of development projects — state, corporate or otherwise — although the benefits may be destined for someone else. There are centers and institutions of decision-making detached from but affecting the local communities. The local area is but one of the arenas or spaces of engagement for development activists and voluntary organizations. The others are the nation state, the interstate systems at the subregional, Asian and global levels, the multilateral institutions and the global corporate structures.

To be effective, voluntary action should take place in all these arenas. Some voluntary organizations operate at all levels simultaneously. Others confine themselves to one arena. But if all voluntary organizations share the same development vision and values, their efforts will converge and achieve their common goals.

Colonialism, imperialism and wars have a way of bringing people closer to one another. They have triggered the feeling of "Asian-ness" among Asians. Unfortunately for the Japanese people, WWII moved Asians toward solidarity against them and their country. The Indochina war gave birth to powerful anti-US people's solidarity movements across the Asia-Pacific. The wounds of war take time to heal and the healing has not been hastened by the behavior of either the US or Japan whose continuing hegemony brings Asian peoples closer to one another.

Asian People's Plan 21

The consensus among the Asian elites that economic growth should be pursued at any cost has been consolidated by the success of the NICs. Governments and big business justify their position by pointing to the economic stagnation and endemic and rising poverty in the region. The elite's idea of growth will likely be the dominant influence in the development processes that will take Asia-Pacific into the next century.

Grass-roots movements and voluntary organizations are challenging the new growth orthodoxy with their own vision and strategies. They are not anti-growth; their alternative development agenda promote equitable and ecologically sound development for the whole region.

In 1988, a year before the UN General Assembly approved the holding of the Earth Summit in Rio de Janeiro in 1992, a Japanese people's alliance proposed a brilliant, forward-looking and innovative idea: People's Plan for the 21st century. The idea is now an Asia-Pacific, if not global, citizens' movement. It was originally proposed by the Pacific-Asia Resource Center (PARC), an action-oriented research, education, and documentation center established in 1973 to promote people-to-people solidarity mainly in Asia-Pacific. The movement is now known as PP21.

PP21 grew out of the need to "produce a vision of the future society which is worth winning together." It counterposes a people-based and people-centered vision of an alternative Asian future to

CHAPTER 6

TRANSNATIONAL DEMOCRACY IN ASIA-PACIFIC

Over the last three decades, democratization from below has crossed local and national frontiers and spread throughout Asia-Pacific. People's movements and other voluntary organizations are now linked regionally by structures and processes they have created over the years.

Before, Asian peoples were linked mainly through structures and mechanisms created from above. People-to-people linkages, mediated by states and inter-state systems, centered on trade, education, culture and sports. They were, and still are, largely bilateral or subregional, such as the Southeast Asia Treaty Organization (SEATO) and its successor, the Association of Southeast Asian Nations (ASEAN). Except for the Asian Games, Asia-wide state-mandated people-to-people contacts are almost nonexistent.

Asia-Pacific citizens' groups and movements are more closely linked to their Northern counterparts than they are to one another. One reason is globalization attending colonialism and modernization. Another is the vastness of the region, with distances between countries magnified by poor communication technology. For instance, it is much easier to communicate or travel between the Philippines and Europe than between the Philippines and India, even though English is widely used in these two countries in official as well as personal communication.

The conference also featured songs, poetry and dances by the different groups. The message of the First Asian Indigenous Women's Conference may be captured in the following song:

Women of Asia
Song of Unity of the First Asian Indigenous Women's Conference
Lyrics by Joji Cariño, Judy Cariño, and Nancy Jouwe
Music by Judy Cariño

Refrain
We are the women of Asia / We are the people of the land
We are the women of Asia / We stand together hand in hand
We work on our native soil / Feel the sweat - from our toil
With the power of our hand / We feed the people of the land.

Dayak, Papua, Rakhain, Chakma / Lest our cultures be forgotten
Kadasan, Lahu, Mamanwa / Bequeath our values to children
Karen Kachin Agta, Puma / Teach them what is right and wrong
Tay, Senoi, Buuman, Ayta / Sons and daughters proud and strong
Igorot, Mangyan, Bangwaon / Our work fills up all our days
Amis, Nhang, Ainu, Higaonon / We walk miles to the market place
Naga, Teduray, Bagobo / Climb the steep hills, plant the trees
Tayal, Seedeg, Tayal, Moro / Mine the earth and dive the seas
We are sisters, wives, and mothers /
We the women are solid and fighting
We provide and care for others / Hearts and minds and spirits uniting
From our wombs they were begotten /
Fists in the air, feet on the earth
Generations of our children / A women's movement on the birth

The United Nations has declared 1993 as the Year for the World's Indigenous Peoples. The First Asian Indigenous Women's Conference was a fitting celebration of this long overdue tribute to one of the prime saviors of the environment.

zations together. War, war-related famine, gross violation of human rights, massive rainforest destruction and large-scale natural disasters were caused or worsened by states, multilateral institutions, such as the World Bank and the Asian Development Bank, and transnational corporations.

Peace movements born during the Vietnam war, far from being exhausted, continue to fuel voluntary citizen action despite the end of the so-called Cold War era. Citizens are mobilizing and pressuring governments to establish a nuclear-weapons-free and demilitarized zone of peace and security. They are particularly worried by the remilitarization of Japan, the continuing military presence of the US in South Korea and elsewhere in the Pacific, and the rising tension resulting from intense economic competition between the US and Japan.

The 1971 war in Bangladesh was another important transboundary issue. It inspired a sense of common humanity and gave rise to citizens' movements inside and outside the country which supported the war victims. Most of the big NGOs in Bangladesh were born during this period. International assistance created a great sense of people-to-people solidarity.

Transnational democracy movements in the Asia-Pacific region are fuelled by massive human-rights violations in countries which follow the path of authoritarian development. Asians have been moved by atrocities in Indonesia in the 1960s and, more recently, the Philippines, Thailand, South Korea, Taiwan, Singapore, Kampuchea under the Polpot regime, Bangladesh, Nepal, Burma, and Tien An Men.

Human-rights movements are at the vanguard of struggles for democracy also because development and environment are fundamentally issues of rights and, therefore, linked to almost every human concern that moves every citizen to voluntary action.

The 1993 UN World Conference on Human Rights held in Vienna brought human-rights groups from all over Asia together. Before the meeting they agreed on a common position. In Vienna, they engaged Asian government delegations in sharp debates, indicating that they can pressure governments into changing their policies. Later, human-rights groups made their presence felt at the meeting of government ministers hosted by the Singapore government, a clear sign that states are forced to respond to pressures from below.

International people's tribunals, a dramatic weapon of human-rights advocates, counter oppression by the geopolitical centers of power in the North. The popular expression of transnational democracy arose out of citizens' frustration with conventional international mechanisms set up to redress injustice.

Bertrand Russell, the noted British philosopher, convened the first international people's tribunal in the late 1960s to investigate allegations that the US was guilty of war crimes in Vietnam. Inspired by the Russell Tribunal, a prominent Italian parliamentarian, Lelio Basso, founded the International League for the Rights of Peoples in the mid-1970s. The League established the Permanent Peoples Tribunal in Rome, creating a body accessible to the peoples of the world whose grievances were ignored by states and international institutions controlled by power elites.

The Permanent Peoples Tribunal has responded to 17 complaints since then. The Asian cases it has taken up include self-determination for Tibet, gross violations of human rights during martial rule in the Philippines, Soviet aggression against Afghanistan, and industrial disasters, such as the massive chemical poisoning in Bhopal, India, and mercury poisoning in Minamata, Japan.

In July 1993, Japanese citizens' groups organized the Tokyo Tribunal to judge the Group of Seven. It was modelled after the 1988 Berlin Permanent Peoples Tribunal which charged the International Monetary Fund and World Bank with acting as agents of global capital and with imposing a variety of intolerable economic burdens on countries of the South. The Tokyo Tribunal charged the US, Japan, Germany, Canada, Great Britain, France and Italy with causing poverty and inequality, and with destroying the environment.

In keeping with the spirit of transnational democracy from below, the Tokyo Tribunal deliberately refrained from rendering a

Popular Education Movement

Across the Asia-Pacific thousands of development workers and citizen volunteers have been working to eradicate illiteracy. But beyond teaching people how to read, write and do numbers, they are generating a popular education movement for people empowerment.

While there have been great advances in the formal educational systems, nearly 1 billion people — 35 percent of the adult population of the world — remain illiterate. Although no exact figures are available, it may be presumed that a significant part of the illiterates are to be found in Asia-Pacific, especially South Asia. UNESCO's goal of education for all still has a long way to go.

Education and training is the core of the software side of development. It is an essential component of every development program or project of both nongovernmental development agencies and grassroots organizations.

The Asia-South Pacific Bureau of Adult Education (ASPBAE) stands out among the NGOs because its main focus is education. Founded in 1964 in Sydney, Australia, following a UNESCO seminar attended by its pioneers, ASPBAE is recognized internationally for its contribution to non-formal adult education.

judgment. Asserting that the privilege was reserved for the peoples of the world, it indicted the G-7 countries based on oral and written testimonies and the knowledge and experience of its panelists.

Citizens' environmental movements strengthen regional democratization from below. Some of the best recent examples are the campaigns to save the Sarawak rainforests, and to stop the Narmada dam project in India, the Pak Mun dam in Thailand, the Three Gorges Dam in China, and the nuclear testing and dumping of hazardous, toxic and nuclear wastes in the South Pacific. The sheer magnitude of impact of the campaigns evokes in the citizens' movements across and beyond the Asia-Pacific a sense of urgency to

ASPBAE's membership base include national associations of adult education, individuals and institutions. By 1988, it counted among its members 14 national associations, 35 institutions and 75 individuals. In its First General Assembly in 1991, hundreds of delegates came representing around 35 countries. ASPBAE is also affiliated to the International Council of Adult Education (ICAE) whose leadership includes outstanding popular educators like Paolo Freire, author of *Pedagogy of the Oppressed.*

Regional and national activities of ASPBAE and its members cover a wide range of concerns. These include peace and human rights, trade-union education, environment, women, youth education, education of indigenous peoples, social awareness, curriculum and pedagogy development, participatory methodologies and many others, including health and drug abuse.

Many other groups in the Asia-Pacific are training and developing an increasing number of popular educators who are capable of galvanizing citizen action around development, environment and human rights issues. Not only do they deliver a basic service to the millions who continue to suffer government neglect, more important, they utilize education as a means to people empowerment.

彬

act and to demonstrate their solidarity with the millions of people affected.

Environmentalism is linked to self-determination, a theme that runs through most of the struggles already cited. Some movements advocate environmentalism within the framework of nationhood. The best example is the Nuclear-Free and Independent Pacific (NFIP), formed in the 1970s and led by citizen activists in the small island states of the Pacific. Citizens are risking their lives to defend the environment. Indigenous peoples and local communities are fighting back, literally lying in the path of bulldozers and logging trucks of powerful interests. Their experiences, successful or failed,

Citizens Resist the Greens

In April 1993, in Malaysia, three Asia-based citizens' networks came together to form the Global Anti-Golf Movement (GAG'M). The new movement was born out of the Conference on Golf Course and Resort Development organized by the Global Network for Anti-Golf Course Action (GNAGA), the Asia-Pacific People's Environment Network (APPEN) and the Asian Tourism Action Network (AN-TENNA) and attended by delegates from Hawaii, Hong Kong, India, Indonesia, Japan, Malaysia, the Philippines and Thailand.

GAG'M was a response to the increasing outcry of many local communities across the globe against the expansion of golf courses everywhere. The new movement calls the attention of citizens around the world to the adverse social and ecological impacts of an ever expanding space for an elitist sport, which powerful business interests are lobbying for inclusion in the Olympic Games.

According to the *Earth Island Journal*, there are about 24,000 golf courses on the earth, 13,600 of which are found in the United States. The *Environmentalist* estimates that 5.9 million acres of our planet's surface are covered by golfing greens. The drive for more golf-course development is spreading to Central and South America and, recently, even to the former communist countries of Eastern Europe. Poland, for example, is being prepared as a haven for multinational investors from the West and golf courses are part of the incentive package.

Ironically, the expansion of golf courses (also called greens) is taking place as land resources and agriculture are more and more severely stressed. Desertification, for example, affects about one-

teach citizens' movements across Asia-Pacific about expanding grassroots democracy.

Broad movements found that they needed institutional structures to link their activities. Different groups formed a string of Asia-wide coalitions, networks, forums and coordinating committees.

The nature of the structures depends on the reasons for forming them, the kind of groups that gravitate toward each other, and

sixth of the world's population, 70 percent of all drylands and one-quarter of the total land area in the world, on top of the degradation of 3.3 billion hectares of rangelands.

The greens expansion is bound to worsen the problem of living space. The golfcourse may look green on the outside but, in reality, it brings a range of damaging effects on local communities and their life-support systems.

The golf industry is a multibillion-dollar enterprise involving transnational corporations in agribusiness, construction, consultancy, sports equipment manufacturing, airlines and hotels, real estate, advertising and public relations, and high finance. Membership in golf courses are expensive. The bulk of the foreign-exchange earnings generated does not stay in the local economy.

Citizen action groups liken the golf industry to the Green Revolution, with the latter's legacy of environmental degradation and falling farmers' income despite increased production. Golf greens are not simply enclaves in micro ecosystems, they are developed through a high input of exotic soil and grass, chemical fertilizers, pesticides, fungicides, weedicides and machinery which pollute the soil, surface and ground water and destroy biodiversity.

Anti-golf citizens' campaigns have rapidly generated widespread public attention. Citizens' groups in Thailand, Hawaii, Indonesia, the Philippines, Japan, India, Nepal, Taiwan, the United Kingdom, Australia and Switzerland launched "World No Golf Day" on 29 April 1993 .

These activities elicited media interest. National newspapers in several countries and regional and international magazines, such as *Newsweek, The New Scientist, The Economist* and *The Ecologist*

the groups' goals, activity cycle, resource requirements and resource availability. Some structures are permanent; many last only as long as the project. The shorter-lived structures have a secretariat lodged in a lead organization or created separately from members of participating organizations.

Long-term groups include the Asian Coalition for Agrarian Reform and Rural Development (ANGOC), the Third World Net-

highlighted the concerns about golf-course development globally.

The most significant perhaps have been the anti-golf activities in Indonesia. A long-standing struggle of farmers in Citeureup, supported by students and lawyers, and local media, against the conversion of vital paddy fields into a golf course by a private company, resulted in a temporary ban on new golf-course development issued by Java authorities. Then in October 1993, several protesting farmers were imprisoned, underlining the human-rights dimension of the golf issue.

In Malaysia, citizen opposition has temporarily stalled the construction of a golf resort by raising the issue of environmental impact. The citizen protestors demanded an environmental impact assessment (EIA) of the project because of its anticipated effects, such as severe soil erosion, siltation and river pollution.

In Hong Kong, environmentalist groups went to court to challenge the developers of the Gary Player-designed Sha Lo Tung Golf Course. The project was stopped on the ground of heritage protection: the golf course would have been built on a parkland.

Inspired by these initial successes, the Global Anti-Golf Movement has set its eyes on other parts of the Asian region. China, Vietnam, Laos and Cambodia are current targets of greens development.

🌿

work, the Asia-Pacific Bureau on Adult Education (ASPBAE), Asia-Pacific Peoples Environmental Network (APPEN), Asian Alliance of Human Rights Organizations, and the Asian Students Associations (ASA). Examples of temporary and more fluid groups include the UNCED coordinating committees, the Asian Development Bank lobby group, the South-North Project for Sustainable Development in Asia, and Sustainable Agriculture Network.

In many cases centralized structures are not necessary to establish Asia-wide links among organizations and movements. Bilateral relationships are sometimes favored over multilateral. Multiple bilateral arrangements and flexible multilateral structures avoid bureaucratization and promote a wider latitude for direct voluntary action.

Obstacles to Democratization

Supranational integration of economic and political power is the biggest impediment to democratization from below. As markets and ecological space diminish, resources and decisions are concentrated in fewer and fewer institutions dominated by the most powerful states and transnational corporations. The result is regionalization. While regionalization can move power away from the traditional international elite, it can also mean hegemony of Japan or more intense Japanese competition with the US which is not about to give up its hold on Asia-Pacific.

The elite consensus that growth should be achieved at any cost means that the social and ecological problems of this century will be magnified several fold in the next. Rapid economic growth will undermine the commitment of Asia-Pacific states to carry out the UNCED agreements. NIC-type industrialization, together with Japanese-type modernization, will further stress the ecological capacity of the region. Asia is still rich in biodiversity and minable resources but will not be able to sustain high-speed growth for long. The region's sink capacity, which remains comparatively large, will not last long either once industrialization goes full steam ahead.

The international power elites have a decided edge over grassroots and citizens' movements in the battle for Asian hearts and minds. The media and all instruments of educating and informing the masses are under elite control. The superhyping campaigns for NIC development in schools, newspapers, television and radio, not to mention the voluminous literature churned out by official development institutions, highlight the citizens' movements' disadvantage.

Citizens' movements, especially at the grass-roots, are handicapped by channels for information exchange which are not only limited but expensive. Access to information has improved a great deal in the past few years due to electronic technology and com-

Nuclear Bomb Tests
in the South Pacific

There was a blinding flash that became a ball of fire. Then the ball of fire formed into a gigantic orange mushroom cloud. Soon the sky turned into blood red. In the following seconds, there was a deafening explosion and then a sudden rushing of a tornado-like wind that twisted trees and sent roofs of houses flying. Later the ash fall from a strange "snow" in the form of pulverized coral and debris.

The people of the Polynesian islands did not know what had happened. Some picked up the dust and tasted it. Others rubbed it in their eyes, wondering if it might cure an old ailment. People walked on it, children had fun playing with it. Soon their skin itched terribly, they became severely nauseous and many lost their hair. Drinking water turned yellow and bitter and poisoned those who drank it.

It was the Polynesians' first taste of the nuclear bomb test. The Americans conducted 66 such nuclear tests at Bikini and Enewatak between 1946 and 1958. The biggest blast of all was that of an H-bomb, codenamed Bravo, on March 1, 1954. A 15-megaton monster, it was 1,000 times stronger than the bomb dropped on Hiroshima.

The French carried out their first nuclear test in French Polynesia in the South Pacific on July 2, 1966. In the next eight years there

puter-based communication systems. But while some voluntary organizations are already hooked up to these systems, many more are not, especially grass-roots groups which cannot afford the cost of installation or whose remote location does not allow them easy access to the systems.

The feverish pace of globalization of development and environment problems underlines the need for more effective communication in order to pool together and organize the scattered responses of different citizens groups. The policies and activities of regional institutions, like the Asian Development Bank, the World Bank,

were 43 more tests.

In the years that followed, people reported cases of radiation sickness, fish poisoning, painful rheumatic condition and leukemia. The Polynesians continue to suffer these effects to this day.

The Polynesians were roused from the quiet of their paradise-like island habitats as the nuclear tests began to take their toll. Popular outrage further fuelled the already boiling issues of independence, self-determination and a nuclear-free Pacific.

The plight of the South Pacific peoples has gained wider public attention in recent years. The entry of Greenpeace dramatized it even more.

On July 10, 1985, the Greenpeace boat, *Rainbow Warrior*, was sunk by a French bomb while docked at the Auckland bay in New Zealand. Fernando Pereira, a Dutch/Portuguese photographer who joined the *Rainbow Warrior* in its South Pacific anti-nuclear campaign, drowned.

The *Rainbow Warrior* was destined for Moruroa, a South Pacific island then a testing ground for French nuclear bombs. The prospect of Polynesians joining the action with their outrigger canoes worried the French government, already under severe pressure from independence movements in the Pacific territories. The bombing of the *Rainbow Warrior* triggered public protests all around the world which almost brought down the Mitterand government.

transnational corporations and interstate bodies must be monitored. Existing action-alert and early-warning systems set up by NGOs cannot yet adequately respond to the increasing demand for timely and accurate information.

Another problem confronting the voluntary sector is its dependency on development assistance from the North. Among both grass-roots movements and development support organizations are those totally dependent on foreign funding. Their dependency gives rise to a number of problems, the most important of which is the loss of autonomy of the recipient organizations. Many donor orga-

Anything Goes for Angry Citizens

Nothing is too puny or comical to stimulate some kind of citizen response.

In the Philippines, which gained fame for its trend-setting citizens' revolution in 1986, a somewhat unusual movement emerged in 1992 which eventually became part of the larger popular movement. It went by the name Alliance 349. The story began with a freak incident.

The Pepsi Cola company, then in the midst of its advertising hype against Coca-Cola, launched a multimillion-peso-prize campaign. Pepsi drinkers could win a million pesos after forming the number 349 from digits embedded under the cork of Pepsi bottles. But something went wrong with the computer program: instead of the originally planned 18 winning entries, the Pepsi computer generated 800,000 which could cost the company some $32 billion. Acknowledging its mistake but obviously unable to pay the price for it, Pepsi made a 500-peso (about $20) "goodwill" offer to all holders of the magic number, amounting to $10 million which was five times the original promotion budget.

nizations impose their own views on how development should proceed in the South. Local organizations' dependency draws them away from opportunities that are available within the country, limiting the possibilities for local resource mobilization. The decline or cutback of foreign assistance will surely magnify this problem.

Civil society is not synonymous with democracy. In civil society there are tyrants, too. And civilian fundamentalism has several expressions, from plain bigotry to communal violence. The phenomenal rise movements inspired by religious fanaticism has begun to threaten and undermine democratization from below. Despite the anti-colonial and anti-modernization overtones of some of them, citizens' movements of this variety cannot provide the kind of spiritual empowerment needed to promote an equitable and sustainable future for humanity.

The "winning" consumers, already savoring the prospect of spending a cool million each (not a few of them winning more than once) would not let Pepsi get away with it. More than 22,000 people holding the 349 number combination have filed civil suits, seeking damages. In addition, 5,200 criminal complaints alleging fraud and deception on the part of Pepsi have also been lodged in court.

Mobilization was feverish. And what began merely as a Lady Luck exercise became a human-rights issue. In face of popular clamor for redress, human-rights organizations willingly obliged.

Neither Pepsi nor the disgruntled former Pepsi drinkers budged.

In June 1993, after a long silence, over 50,000 Filipinos took to the streets again to challenge the national-development program of the newly elected Ramos government. Alliance 349 joined in, spicing up the march with a Mardi Gras procession, a band, slogans and placards and streamers that stood out in the predominantly leftist crowd. The strange mix of Alliance 349 demands and communist calls lent a surreal air to the event.

❧

Nongovernmental and people's organizations also have their share of imperfections. In some ways they mirror the oppressive relations in society they have been striving all these years to change. Probably because the struggle for a better world is so complex, NGOs sometimes get lost in a web of problems that confuse their identity and undermine their core values, such as autonomy, pluralism, diversity, closeness to the grass-roots, bottom-up perspective and volunteerism.

Some organizations build layers and layers of bureaucratic structures and end up behaving like state institutions. Some self-appointed leaders behave like politicians and bureaucrats, pretend to represent that loosely defined entity called the NGO community, and claim jurisdiction over citizens and territories. This behavior is called state substitution.

Organizations are also guilty of parallelism. In their frustration with state policies, they go about their business as though government did not exist. Having set up substitute structures, they think that they can make an impact on development in spite of the government. A variant of this problem is also called politics of avoidance where voluntary organizations tend to mind only their own narrow turf and leave the big decisions to politicians and their corporate allies.

Then there are spurious organizations which unscrupulous individuals set up to raise funds in the guise of promoting the common good only to run away with the money. There are also government-organized NGOs (GONGOs) and donor-organized NGOs (DONGOs). GONGOs are usually set up to make money for certain corrupt officials. DONGOs are organized by donors as a means of imposing their own policies and programs. BONGOs or business-organized NGOs, as distinct from genuine corporate philanthrophies, are organized by business people as tax and import-duty shelters.

Civil society flourishes in pluralism and diversity. Conflicts of agenda and multiple strategies and approaches add color and fire to citizens' movements. And for as long as groups can demonstrate a fairly high threshold of tolerance for differences, there is no doubt they will overcome or avoid "NGO diseases" and eventually converge toward a common higher goal.

Looking to the Future

The evolving scenario for transnational democracy in the Asia-Pacific region is difficult to paint. It is certain that there is no stopping the growth rollercoaster and that advocates of an equitable and sustainable Asian future will be hard put to redirect the growth trajectory. Yet Asian citizens can convert problems into opportunities and assert an alternative vision for a 21st-century Asia-Pacific.

One opportunity for the citizens' movements is the commitment made by Asian states and governments to carry out all the UNCED agreements. Monitoring compliance by governments at the national and regional levels is a crucial task that can complement grass-roots initiatives seeking to promote a just and ecologically sound development.

Citizens' movements increase the pressure on governments to draw up a common regional or subregional plan to calibrate modernization to the limits of the region's natural environment. Appropriate scaling of development requires a shared definition of industrial and trading niches, a common but differentiated responsibility for curbing transboundary pollution and dumping of hazardous, toxic and nuclear wastes, and a plan for protecting and restoring biodiversity and the health of the upland, lowland, coastal and marine ecosystems. The growing ecological agriculture movements should play a key role in pressuring and business corporations governments because rapid industrialization is killing agriculture.

Citizens must press for structural adjustment that will harmonize comparative advantages, offset relative resource scarcities and correct inequalities and imbalances within and among nations. A cut-and-share arrangement in production and consumption should be worked out among the haves and the have-nots of Asia-Pacific.

As subregional trading blocs will eventually consolidate at the regional level, citizens' movements must vigorously advocate better trade terms for the time being and an alternative trading system strategically.

Although difficult to build, an alternative trading system that is linked to grass-roots activities must be established to provide the citizens' movements' perspective and vision in current and future negotiations among the Asian states. A people-oriented "altertrade" system not only promotes fair trade but ensures that communities and countries trade only their surpluses after meeting their basic needs and services. Today, countries and transnational corporations are trading goods and services at the expense of local communities and their life-support systems. This trading system weakens the capacity of local communities for self-determination and destroys the ecosystems upon which these communities depend for their living.

People-to-people trade is a direct counterpoint to the global trading system. The International Federation for Alternative Trade has significant achievements in promoting people-to-people trade. Some Japanese citizens' groups trade in organically grown bananas, linking producers in the Philippines directly to Japanese consumers in an equitable and environment-friendly relationship. These successes suggest what is possible within the limits of an unequal global trading system.

Trade wars in Asia-Pacific among the rich and powerful can be tamed by citizen action up to a point. They cannot be prevented by simple recourse to the package of liberal policies that aim to pry open the economies of Asian countries, as proposed by the IMF, the World Bank, the Asian Development Bank and transnational corporations.

Several Asian voluntary groups are lobbying directly against the policies and activities of multilateral development institutions and transnational corporations. The Uruguay Round of the General Agreement on Tariffs and Trade (GATT) lobby is an outstanding example. Asian groups have mounted a similar campaign to take on the Asian Development Bank.

Citizens' movements, led by human rights, peace and anti-nuke movements, go beyond trade issues and are pressuring governments to establish a regional zone of peace, security, neutrality and prosperity. Their activities can be effective not only against the intensification of trade wars but also against the eruption of open military conflicts.

Asia-Pacific can be transformed from a region of instability to a zone of peace and security based on demilitarization, respect for the sovereignty and dignity of peoples and environmental sustainability. The change will happen only if citizens' movements use their collective voice and power to define new terms of engagement with states, interstate systems and the business corporations.

The world that favored the rise of the Asian economic "miracles" is no more. What confronts the citizens of Asia-Pacific is a planet whose economic and ecological space may soon disappear. Citizens must continue to engage in voluntary action and strive for an alternative path to a common Asian future.

ANNOTATED BIBLIOGRAPHY

The American Council for Voluntary International Action (ACVIA).
1991 InterAction: Member Profiles. New York: ACVIA, 1991.
A directory of 125 member organizations of InterAction involved in international humanitarian assistance.

Ampo: Japan-Asia Quarterly Review. Vol. 18, nos.2-3, 1986; vol.
19, No. 1, 1987; vol. 19, no. 2, 1987; vol. 19, no. 3, 1987;
vol. 20, no. 3 (series no. 77); vol. 22, nos. 2 & 3 (series nos.
84, 85); vol. 23, no. 2 (series no. 87); vol. 24, no. 1, 1993;
vol. 24, no. 2, 1993.
Covers a wide range of issues concerning Japan and Asia-Pacific.

Asia Monitor Resource Center (AMRC). *Min-Ju No-Jo: South Korea's
New Trade Unions.* Hongkong: AMRC, 1988.
An account of the struggles of the South Korean workers.

Asian Development Bank (ADB). *Annual Report.* Manila: ADB,
1992.
Source of data on the Bank's developing member countries and
trends in Asia-Pacific, particularly urbanization.

Asiaweek. May 19, 1993.
Contains articles on Indonesia.

Arena Bulletin: Asian Exchange. Vol. 9, nos. 1/2. May 1993.
Provides a broad survey of social movements in Asia-Pacific.

Bello, Walden. *People & Power in the Pacific: The Struggle for the
Post-Cold War Order.* London, USA, Amsterdam: Pluto Press,
Institute for Food and Development Policy (Food First),
Transnational Institute (TNI), 1992.

An analysis of the power configuration in the Pacific, with recommendations for state policy and popular intervention.

_____ and Stephanie Rosenfeld. *Dragons in Distress: Asia's Miracle Economies in Crisis*. England: Clays Ltd, St Ives plc, 1992.
A powerful analysis exposing the myths and realities surrounding the "economic miracles" of the NICs.

_____. *Toward a People's Pacific*. New York: The People-Centered Development Forum, 1992.
A summary of Bello's People and Power in the Pacific, with stress on his three points of intervention: 1) an Asia-Pacific Technoeconomic Bloc; 2) an Alternative Security System; and 3) a Congress of Asian NGOs.

Brown, Michael and John May. *The Greenpeace Story*. New York: Dorling Kindersley, 1991.
An account of Greenpeace activities in the South Pacific, particularly in the anti-nuclear test campaign.

Clark, John. *Democratizing Development: The Role of Voluntary Organizations*. London: Earthscan, 1991.
Tackles the subject of voluntary organizations and their contribution to and impact on development theory and practice.

Cordillera Women's Education and Resource Center, Inc. (CWERC). *Proceedings of the First Asian Indigenous Women's Conference*. Baguio: CWERC, 1993.
A resource on the different situations of indigenous peoples in Asia and the activities of Asian indigenous women's groups.

Crawshaw, Josie. "Wallow in the Backwaters or Sink in the Mainstream? No! Navigate New Waters!" Presented at a conference organized by the Maori Women's Welfare League, Darwin, Australia, 1993.
Discusses issues affecting self-determination.

Development Support Service of the IRED Partners in Asia (DSS:Asia). *The Colombo Statement of Asian NGOs & People's Organisations on People's Empowerment in Asia.* Document No. 01. Colombo: DSS:Asia, 1992.
A comprehensive position on various issues affecting people's empowerment, signed by the Asian colloquium participants, including Serrano.

The Ecologist. Vol. 22, no. 4. July/August 1992; vol. 23, no. 2 March/April 1993; vol. 23, no. 3, May/June 1993.
Provides in-depth analyses of various development, environment and human-rights issues.

Ekins, Paul. *A New World Order: Grassroots Movements for Global Change.* London, New York: Routledge, Chapman and Hall, Inc., 1992.
Argues for a paradigm shift and the crucial role of grass-roots movements in the emerging world order.

Fernandes, Rubem Cesar. "Back & Forward to 'Civil Society'." Written for the Working Group on Poverty, Economy and Environment of Unit III, World Council of Churches.
Highlights the role of civil society in current global changes.

Food and Agriculture Organization of the United Nations (FAO). *Directory of Non-Governmental Organizations for Rural Development.* Rome: FAO, 1985.
Profiles 500 rural NGOs of which 105 are in Asia-Pacific.

Hill, Helen. "Non-Governmental Organizations in the South Pacific Region: Towards a Typology for Identifying Learning Needs." Paper presented to the Commonwealth Association for the Education and Training of Adults (CAETA) Conference, Nottingham, UK, 1993.

_____. "Peoples' Organization and International Issues, Towards a Typology for North and South." Presented to a conference of The Australian Sociological Association, Adelaide, Australia, 1992.

_____. *Directory of Australian NGOs.* May 15, 1993. Includes 192 NGOs.

Ho Shuet Ying. *Taiwan — After a Long Silence.* Hong Kong: Asia Resource Center, 1990.
An account of democratic resurgence in Taiwan.

Hodgkinson, Virginia A., Richard W. Lyman et al. *The Future of the Nonprofit Sector.* San Francisco: Independent Sector, 1989.
A good reference for global trends in the voluntary sector.

Holloway, Richard. "Civil Society — the Non-profit Private Sector: Trying to Categorize It in Bangladesh." Presented to UNICEF, Dhaka, Bangladesh, April 1993.
Presents a neat and detailed typology of civil society. Bases some of its arguments on Chapter 6 of David Korten's *Getting into the 21st Century —Voluntary Action and the Global Agenda,* but goes beyond the narrow NGO frame. The best attempt yet at taxonomy of civil society organizations.

Hongkong Trade Union Education Centre (HTUEC) and Asia Monitor Resource Center Ltd., *At the Crossroads: Hong Kong Independent Trade Union Movement and the International Trade Secretariats (ITS):Report on the August 9-10, 1988 Conference.* Hong Kong: HTUEC, 1988.

Human Development Report 1993. Delhi: Oxford University Press, 1993.
Gives a global picture of performance by UN member countries in terms of a set of quality-of-life indicators and an assessment of NGO impact.

Hunt, Janet, Russel Rollason, Edna Ross and Robert Salter. *One World or...None: Making the Difference*. Australia: Australian Council for Overseas Aid and Pluto Press Austria, 1989.
Calls for concerted global action on issues affecting human development and environment.

International Campaign for Ecological Justice in Indonesia. *Down to Earth*. No. 20/21. June 1993.
Reports on the environment movement in Indonesia.

The International Peoples Tribunal to Judge the G-7. "Indictment." Tokyo, Japan, July 3-4, 1993.
Summarizes and analyzes the impact of structural adjustment and the responsibility of G-7 countries. Includes testimonies of experts from different countries.

Japanese Working for A Better World: Grassroots Voices & Access Guide to Citizens' Groups in Japan. San Francisco: Honnoki USA, 1992.
Profiles 47 outstanding individuals involved in various voluntary activities. It also contains the Access Guide to 754 citizens' groups addressing environment and development issues.

Keating, Michael. "Main Outline: North America Chapter-CIVICUS." July 16, 1993.
Provides a sample reference for the CIVICUS Asia Report.

Korten, David. *Getting to the 21st Century — Voluntary Action and the Global Agenda*. Connecticut: Kumarian Press, 1990.
Criticizes the conventional development paradigm and describes the role of voluntary action in forging and realizing an alternative vision for the 21st century.

Leung Wing-yue *Smashing the Iron Rice Pot*. Hongkong: Asia Monitor Resource Center Ltd, 1988.
A general reference on the situation of workers and trade unions in China's market socialism.

Lippmann, Lorna. *Generations of Resistance: Aborigines Demand Justice.* Australia: Longman Cheshire Pty Ltd, 1992.
Historical and present-day accounts of the aboriginal movement in Australia.

Lokayan Bulletin. Delhi. November-December 1991,9:6.
Reports on grass-roots activities in India.

Lu Ping. *China: A Moment of Truth.* Hongkong: Asia Monitor Resource Center Ltd, 1990.
An account of the Tian An Men incident and the role played by the workers.

McCarthy, Kathleen D., Virginia A. Hodgkinson and Russy D. Sumariwalla. *The Nonprofit Sector in the Global Community: Voices from Many Nations.* San Francisco: Jossey-Bass, Inc., 1991.
Contains essays on Japan by Tadashi Yamamoto, on India by Anil K. Gupta, Indonesia by Onny S. Prijono, Singapore by Paul P.L. Cheung, and China by Junhai Zheng.

Morales, Horacio Jr. *A Call for People's Development.* Manila: National Council of Churches in the Philippines, 1990.
A collection of essays on issues confronted by Philippine NGOs and POs.

Mukul. *Against The Stream: India's Economic Crisis and Workers' Alternatives.* New Delhi: Charu, 1992.

National Campaign for Housing Rights (NCHR). *Sapping India — Sapping the Indian people: The Impact of the IMF Structural Adjustment Package on Housing and Living Conditions in India.* Bombay: NCHR, 1992.

National Geographic. Vol. 183, no. 5. May 1993.
Contains data on Nauru.

Noguchi, Mary Goebel. "The Rise of the Housewife Activist." *Japan Quarterly.* July-September 1992, pp. 339-51.
Deals with a new trend in Japan and gives the profiles of six leading housewives.

de Oliveira, Rosiska Darcy and Fatima Vianna Thais. *Population Danger: Sex, Lies and Misconceptions.* Rio de Janeiro, 1993.
A good reference on women's positions on various issues.

Organisation for Economic Co-operation and Development (OECD). *Directory of Non-Governmental Environment and Development Organisations in OECD Member Countries.* Paris: OECD, 1992.
Contains profiles of 37 organizations in Canada, 32 in Japan and 77 in the United States.

O'Connel, Brian, ed. *America's Voluntary Spirit: A Book of Readings.* New York: The Foundation Center, 1983.

The Organizing Committee for People's Plan for the 21st Century (PP21). *From Hope to Action: The Alliance of People.* Bangkok: PP21, 1992.

Philippine Rural Reconstruction Movement (PRRM). *Bataan: A Case on Ecosystem Approach to Sustainable Development in the Philippines.* Quezon City: PRRM, 1992.
Argues for a sustainable district development strategy, a contribution of PRRM to the South-North Project on Sustainable Development in Asia.

Project for Ecological Recovery (PER). *The Future of People and Forests in Thailand After the Logging Ban.* Bangkok: PER, 1992.
A case study contributed to the South-North Project on Sustainable Development in Asia.

Sahabat Alam Malaysia. *Directory of Environmental NGOs In The Asia Pacific Region*. Kuala Lumpur: APPEN, 1983. Profiles 330 organizations in Asia-Pacific.

Samaj Parivartana Samudaya, Federation of Voluntary Organisations for Rural Development - Karnataka (FEVORD-K), Action Committee for Protection of Common Lands (ACPCL), Citizens for Democracy - Karnataka and Jana Vikas Andolan. *Janaaranya: People's Participation in the Management of Natural Resources.* Dharwad and Karnataka (JVA-K)B'lore. Bangalore: Samaj Parivartana Samudaya, Federation of Voluntary Organisations for Rural Development - Karnataka (FEVORD-K), Action Committee for Protection of Common Lands (ACPCL), Citizens for Democracy - Karnataka and Jana Vikas Andolan, 1991.

Saunders, Malcolm and Ralph Summy. *The Australian Peace Movement: A Short History.* Canberra: Peace Research Centre Australian National University, 1986.

Serrano, Isagani R. *On Civil Society.* A Monograph Series. Quezon City: Philippine Rural Reconstruction Movement, 1993.

Society for Participatory Research in Asia (SPRA). *Holding Together: Collaborations and Partnerships in the Real World.* New Delhi: SPRA, 1991.

Tandon, Rajesh. "Citizen Action: Future Challenges. " Presented at Managing Change Asian Workshop of Ashoka Foundation, Calcutta, India, March 31-April 2, 1993.

Tandon, Rajesh. "Civil Society, The State and Roles of NGOs." New Delhi, August 1991.

_____. "General Reflections on the Status and Issues of Civil Society in South Asia."

_____. "Adult Education, Cultural Development and Social Movements: The Contemporary Challenge." Presented at International Seminar on Educational and Cultural Development in Local Communities, Aranjuez, Spain, April 27-30, 1993.

_____. "The Role of Voluntary Action in Contemporary Context:Implications for Institutional Development." Presented at the seminar on the above theme held in Orissa, India, May 18-19, 1993.

Tandon's papers are the source of many of the main ideas in this book.

Third World Resurgence. No. 16, December 1991; no. 27, November 1992; no. 33, May 1993.

Deals with a wide range of development and environment issues.

Transnational Institute. "A Directory of Non-Governmental Organizations in Developing Asia and Pacific." Amsterdam, The Netherlands. 1991.

A partial list of NGOs involved in agriculture.

United Nations. *Earth Summit Agenda 21: The United Nations Programme of Action from Rio.* New York: United Nations Department of Public Information, 1992.

_____. *In Our Hands: Directory of Non-Governmental Organisations Accredited to the United Nations Conference on Environment and Development.* New York: The UNCED Secretariat-NGO Unit, 1992.

A directory of 1,420 NGOs accredited to UNCED, including 289 from the Asia-Pacific.

_____. *Earth Summit: Convention on Climate Change.* New York: United Nations Conference on Environment and Development, 1992.

A framework convention on how to stabilize the global climate system, signed by 154 UN member countries present at the Rio Earth Summit.

_____. *Earth Summit: Convention on Biological Diversity.* New York: United Nations Conference on Environment and Development, 1992.
A framework on how to arrest the loss of plant and animal species and restore biodiversity, signed by 154 UN member countries present at the Rio Earth Summit.

Walker, Ranginui and William Sutherland, eds. *The Pacific: Peace, Security and the Nuclear Issue.* Tokyo: Zed Books Ltd. and The United Nations University, 1988.
Deals with peace and security issues in Asia-Pacific.

WALHI. *Mistaking Plantations for the Indonesia's Tropical Forest.* Jakarta: WALHI, 1992.
A case study contributed to the South-North Project on Sustainable Development in Asia.

Weerackody, Chamindra. *An Attempt at NGO-PO Networking: A Sri Lankan Experience.* Document No. 10. Colombo: Development Support Service of the IRED Partners in Asia (DSS:Asia), December 1992.

World Development Report 1992: Development and the Environment. New York: Oxford University Press, 1992.
Discusses the global status of development and environment. Useful for discussions of issues relevant to Asia-Pacific.

World Development Report 1993: Investing in Health. New York: Oxford University Press, 1993.

Yamamoto, Tadashi. "The Survey on Non-Governmental Underpinnings of the Emerging Asia-Pacific Regional Community (Draft Proposal)." Presented to Japan Center for International Exchange, Tokyo, Japan, February 15, 1993.
Includes a comprehensive list of directories of NGOs and philanthropic organizations.

_____. *Cooperative Activities and Networks of Non-Profit Organizations in the Asia-Pacific Region.* Research paper, Seoul, Korea, 1993.

_____. *Preliminary List of Basic Reference: The Survey on Nongovernmental Underpinnings of the Emerging Asia-Pacific Regional Community.* Part of above research proposal.

Yokota, Katsumi. *I, Among Others.* Yokohama: Seikatsu Club Seikyo, 1991.
A story of the Seikatsu Club Cooperative Movement in Kanagawa Prefecture and the author's role in it.

Zivetz, Laurie et al. *Doing Good: The Australian NGO Community.* Sydney: Allen & Unwin Pty Ltd, 1991.

❦

Annex 1

CIVIL SOCIETY, THE STATE AND THE ROLE OF NGOS
- -

By Rajesh Tandon

Introduction

The decade of the 1980s brought development NGOs into the centre of discourse, policy and programming of national and international development institutions and aid agencies. Yet, much of the conceptualization of this phenomenon, both by NGOs themselves and those interested in them, remained inadequate. Note the following trends:

❖ New democratic regimes (like the government in Chile) are calling for "dismantling" of NGOs, as state agencies take over.

❖ Most donors in Europe and North America look at NGOs as transitory, serving a limited purpose for a limited time; then moving on or dissolving themselves. Support for institution-building of NGOs is rather rare and limited.

Many ideas in this paper have been jointly developed with PRIA colleagues (especially Anil Chaudhary and Suneeta Dhar) during our collective work over the past few years.

Discussions with and reflections of several colleagues on a previous draft of this paper have further enriched my analysis. I am thankful to Dave Brown, Francisco Vio Grossi, Michael Bratton, Jane Covey, Paul Wangoola, John Gaventa, Martha Farrell, Mark Leach and Rob Hollister.

❖ Political and bureaucratic elites in many countries of the South are setting up NGO-like institutions (or GONGOs) under State and/or Party control with a view to access resources.

❖ Bi- and Multi-lateral aid agencies are eager to directly fund NGOs as inexpensive service-delivery mechanisms for diverting resources away from "wasteful" and expensive government agencies.

❖ The appeals for institutional pluralism in Eastern Europe as a contribution to democracy gets bogged into private economic enterprise on the one hand, and multiparty politics on the other.

These trends, in debate and practice, seem to be based on a particular view of NGOs and what is their role in the contemporary context. In this paper, these underlying conceptualizations of NGOs and their roles are critiqued and an alternative formulation is presented.

Current Approaches

Recent conceptualization of the growing strength, visibility and importance of the NGOs engaged in promoting development have tended to create an impression that NGOs, voluntary organizations and development institutions are essentially representing the *third* sector. A series of studies, documents and proclamations have resulted in the emerging theorization of the growing importance of the *third* sector. In this framework, the Government becomes the first sector and the corporations or the business the *second* sector (see e.g., Weisbord, 1975; Douglas, 1983; Van Til, 1988; O'Neil, 1989; etc.).

This conceptualization tends to emphasize the importance of recognizing the contributions of the *third* sector, composed of voluntary organizations, development institutions, neighborhood groups, citizen's initiatives, etc. in strengthening a variety of democratic practices, values and traditions in the society. Some theorists have even gone to the extent of articulating the pre-eminent role of the actors of the *third* sector in the emergence and ensuring of democracies in modern nation states (Hyden, 1983; Diamond, et. al., 1989; O'Neil, 1989; Bratton, 1989). While such formulations further demostrate the significance of NGOs, they inadequately explain the underlying reasons for the same. There is a need for a closer look at this theorization in order to develop a better appreciation of what institutions, associations, networks of this so-called "third" sector do represent in our societies.

The First Sector

The first question is to examine whether the Government, or the State in its modern conceptualization, really represents that primacy — the *first* sector. Historically, since the second world war, a modern concept of nation-state has been imposed on many newly independent countries of the South. Trying to overcome the heritage of the colonial rule, these countries embraced a concept of State which was alien to their social, cultural and political milieu (Rothchild and Chazan, 1988). However, within the forty years, in many countries of the South, the State has become a dominant actor. It is not only regulating macro, political and global relations but also determining the manner in which the relationships across families, communities and institutions will be managed. This may tend to create an impression that the State is the primary actor in the contemporary societies. However, the reality on the ground is not necessarily so.

The most telling example of this comes from Africa, where the continuous process of erosion of the legitimacy and power of the State can be witnessed in country after country over the last decade. State apparatus has become fragile, incapable of coherent management of national economy and politics and certainly not respected or accepted by the citizens (Hyden, 1983; Diamond et.al 1989; Rothchild and Chazan, 1988).

Despite signs of powerful and ever expanding State in many Asian countries, the reality on the ground is also quite different.

Large sections of people and many segments of society continue to remain outside the purview of the State. It's policies, agencies and agents have lost legitimacy with large sections of society. Pervasive black market economies and subsistence survival economies are merely an illustration of this disengagement from the State (Rothchild and Chazan, 1988).

The continuous movement between a military dictatorship and a representative form of governance in many countries of Latin America seems to also indicate that the State has not yet acquired the kind of primacy that the theorists provide in their conceptualization of the State as the *first* sector.

The Second Sector

The second difficulty comes in characterizing the business or the corporate world, or the market economy, as the *second* sector in our societies.

First of all, many countries in the South, and increasingly countries in the North too, witness informal economies and sectors which are not hooked to the national or international formal economy. We also witness the large presence of self-employed, family economic enterprises and activities, which can hardly be construed as a corporation, or for that matter, conceptualized to share the same dynamics, culture and perspective as the modern corporate world.

Despite wishes to the contrary, the market economy of many countries in the South, and more recently several countries in the North, continues to show severe distortions and imperfections. This generates the problematic of equating economic development with performance of the market. Certainly, the dominant actors in this sector, the corporate institutions, and multi-national corporations, do not necessarily represent the totality of the economic activities carried out in most countries of the South, and increasingly in the countries of the North, too. So, it is difficult to call the "market sector" the *second* sector. Not only is it problematic to call the State as the *first* sector, and business as the *second*, but it is also inadequate to imply "residual" or "left-over" (whatever is not State and not business) as the *third* sector of NGOs, citizen associations, and neighborhood and community organizations.

In order to understand the role of NGOs, voluntary institutions and associations, citizen's initiatives, neighborhood groups, development organizations, etc. in contemporary society, we need to approach the question of these institutions from a different perspective. We need to *understand the relationship between the State and Civil Society* in order to situate the role of NGOs and voluntary development organizations in that context. This will help us move beyond the "residual" conceptualization of such institutions.

State-Centric

It is interesting to note that over the last fifty years most theorizing and conceptualization in political science, political economy and sociology has been focused on definitions, re-definitions and re-formulations of the State on the question of governance. This governance has been equated with the functioning of Governments. Very little thinking has been done on the question of Civil Society (Bratton, 1991). This is symptomatic of the growing dominance of the State in defining the paradigms of development and the frameworks of relationships in contemporary societies.

The State also became equated with a geo-political configuration following the second World War. Yet, prior to the second World War, or, even prior to the colonial rule, centuries of culture and communities continued to exist and flourish in different parts of the world without the modern concept of State. What provided the basis for the generation of science, technology, culture, art, music, education, etc. in these communities? Obviously, it was the result of the configuration of *Civil Society*.

Civil Society

In the contemporary sense, with the pre-eminent dominance of the State and its agencies in many countries of the South, it is very difficult to define Civil Society, unless we make reference to those historical contexts and dimensions of Civil Society. As we see in many African countries, with the withdrawal or the withering away of the State, the rich associational life of the communities provides the basis for survival and growth of individuals, families and communities (Bratton, 1989).

The concept, structure and practice of the modern State appears to be an alien experience for many societies of the South. The colonial rule followed by imposition of the "modern" State resulted in a disconnectedness between people and governance in such societies (Rothchild and Chazan, 1988). Post-colonial ruling elites of these countries then attempted to consolidate State power. But the gap between the State and the people continued. The State was seen as the unifying structure of governance of geographical and political entities called nation-states. The experience of the form of governance in Europe and North America was thus imposed on the countries of the South as a method of ensuring global interlinkages and continued political and economic dominance of the North over the South. The nationalist fervour of newly independent countries of the South reinforced the tendency to concentrate in the State (and its apparatus) all material, institutional and ideological resources.

Dominance of the State

The State, so conceptualized, plays an increasingly dominant role in determining every aspect of existence of the families and the individuals in contemporary societies. The State makes macro-economic policies; it determines law and order; it has taken over functions of education and health care; it focuses on issues of agricultural development; it has performed tasks of industrial development.

In many situations, as the State begins to acquire greater role, it begins to take over economic, political, cultural and social functions which were till then played within Civil Society. It began to regulate markets, fix prices and costs; it began to define incomes; it began to provide employment and jobs; it regulated currencies, money supply, capital, etc.; it took over functions of art, music and culture; it took over education; it took over health care; it began to play an increasingly overpowering and overarching role in contemporary societies.

Consequences

Several consequences occurred with this predominance of the State. The *first* consequence, which is most evident from the recent experiences of Eastern Europe, is the *dismantling of Civil Society*. Historically rooted associations, neighborhood organizations, citizen initiatives, voluntary organizations disappeared systematically. They were viewed as "obstacles" to progress, or "enemies" of the State, and were slowly replaced by various agencies and departments of the State intending to perform similar functions.

Struggle for the expansion of colonial rule in countries (like India) was resisted by the associations of Civil Society, be they tribal organizations or citizen groups. Thus, such formations were seen as "enemies" of the colonial State. With the end of colonial rule, the form of governance established before Independence continued in countries like India. More importantly, the attitudes and perspectives which informed governance during colonial rule continued to define the practice of governance in newly independent countries of the South. These perspectives and attitudes continued to view institutions of Civil Society as "obstacles" to (at best), or enemies of (at worst) the State and it's agencies.

Where the power of the State and its reach did not go up to the grass-roots, the associational life of poor, distant rural communities continued to survive and thrive, as can be seen in many countries of the South (in tribal and rural areas and remote mountain regions). This dismantling of the institutions of Civil Society became a hallmark of establishing the dominance and the pre-eminence of the State.

The *second* consequence of this was *de-legitimization or de-recognition of old institutions of Civil Society*, which once played similar functions now being performed by the agencies of the State. Thus whenever institutions within Civil Society continued to play the role of providing education or health care or governance, these institutions were questioned and de-legitimized by the newly emerging institutions and actors under the sponsorship of the State. The State in seeking its own legitimization did not tolerate any other form or basis of legitimization in society.

In one way or the other, traditional education practices, histori-cally-rooted health care practices within communities, institutions of local self-governance, etc. were de-legitimized and de-recognized, as the State and its agencies began to take over those functions. Undermining their material base and taking over their "jurisdic-tion" were the two dominant strategies by which the State induced this de-legitimation. In the face of popular resistance to such at-tempts at de-legitimation of local institutions in many countries of the South, the State attempted to play similar roles under the guise of "voluntary" organizations. Thus in a country like India, many State sponsored voluntary organizations — GONGOs or Govern-ment NGOs as we call them — emerged in the place of the de-legitimized and de-recognized traditional institutions of Civil Soci-ety performing similar functions in the community (PRIA, 1989).

A *third* consequence of this was to "homogenize" policies, programmes, perspectives and solutions. While institutions of Civil Society responded to the unique social, cultural, political, economic, geographical and ecological milieu of their communities, the State, out of necessity, began to create *uniform* policies, structures, prac-tices, approaches, officials, etc. This uniformity resulting from a desire for universalization, has led to homogenization of models, ap-proaches, practices, structures and programmes.

One of the major consequences of this homogenization has been the de-recognition, de-legitimization and *dismantling of social diversity* and pluralism from our societies. Bio-diversity is essential to the survival of the life on this planet; social diversity and plural-ism are critical elements in the survival of vibrant societies and com-munities of human beings (Brown 1991). Homogenization of edu-cational approaches, homogenization of health programmes, ho-mogenization of economic models, homogenization of dress, lan-guage, music, etc., led to a steady decline of social diversity. This has significantly undermined the capacities of communities and societies to deal with diverse situations and contexts.

A parallel trend of this homogenization within the countries is the growing homogenization internationally, as the Governments continue to be linked to each other internationally. In this last decade of the 20th century, we are witnessing a phenomenon that growing internationalization of economies and the linkages across the Governments is resulting in the growing homogenization of culture and the destruction of social diversity in art, music, education, health-care, economic development, agriculture, textile, pottery etc. etc.

Fourthly, the ordinary citizens began to be viewed as, and become, mere "consumers." Instead of continuing their role as citizens, with engagement in governance and community life, with being actors in and producers of culture, economy, society, people became mere "consumers" of culture, products and policies. The active citizen was socialized into a passive consumer and lost the civic and political role of citizenship. The State bureaucracy then treats citizens as "clients," passively receiving development produced by the State.

A *fifth* consequence of the growing dominance of the State has been the growing power of the bureaucracy. Official structures, procedures, mechanisms, institutions and officials themselves begin to acquire a life of their own beyond the political perspective of the ruling elite. The power of the bureaucracy to control, to regulate, and to be rigid has been variously experienced and numerously documented over the last fifty years (Hyden, 1983). It is interesting that the government bureaucracy functions in almost the same way, be it America, or the Soviet Union or India or Nigeria. This results in the preeminent and dominating role of the bureaucracy, which evolves it's own interest of perpetuation and maintenance of the status quo. In countries of the South, with high unemployment rates, public bureaucracy becomes an avenue for economic mobility and in many cases the only possible jobs that are available. As a result, getting into public bureaucracy and remaining there becomes the major dream of large numbers of people in contemporary societies, thereby further strengthening its perpetuation.

Over a period of time, bureaucrats defy their political masters, as well as control, regulate, ignore and ridicule the public they are expected to serve. Public bureaucracy acquires a life, a culture, a continuity and an inertia of its own; most of all, it lacks accountability, flexibility, responsiveness and a commitment for collective good. This is perhaps as valid for India as it is for the U.S.A. (see recent report of Kettering Foundation, 1991).

Why the State

So the question really is: Why did the State become so powerful? And why do various theories and conceptualizations of State intervention continue to be so popular?

Firstly, it is important to recognize that the growth of modern capitalism and market economy has always relied heavily on interventions of the State. It is a myth that market economy and modern capitalism means "no" State intervention. Macro policies and external relationships need to be managed by the State in a manner which creates conditions for the rise of capitalist economy. A strong State is therefore needed for the close nexus between the State and the corporate world in a contemporary context (Miliband, 1969). National interest then gets equated with the interests of the State and its ruling forces. The interests of the masses (and subordinate classes) have to take a subsidiary position within this national interest.

Secondly, most proponents of State intervention and the dominant role of the State argued for the use of a "public" instrument to deal with the problems of the newly independent societies forty-fifty years ago.

The question of poverty; the question of inequality and access to and control over resources, the question of inequality in terms of education and health care, income, consumption, shelter; the question of oppression and marginalization all needed to be dealt with through a "public" instrument, which had the legitimacy of the entire populace. The material resources and coercive apparatus were thus controlled by the State to promote such "public" good. The State, in the form of a Parliamentary Democracy in some cases, and the preeminence of a single party in some other cases, was seen as the vehicle to bring about social and economic equality, development and growth.

After 50 years of State intervention in a country like India, it is not clear whether that inequality has increased, decreased or remained the same. It is also not clear whether the State has been able to play the role it was intended to - that of bringing common public good to largest number of masses.

Many countries adopted a single party rule after independence. In the absence of space for dissent, or an alternative point of view, for a different formulation of reality and it's underlying causes, for varied perspectives on a desirable future, no single party, even if it is the Marxist party, can continue to represent aspirations of all the people over a period of time.

The situation becomes all the more difficult in Parliamentary democratic form of governance where the leadership is to be expected to play a role for the common public good. Yet in these forms of governance as well, the State represents a confluence of political and economic interests which need not necessarily represent the interests of the poor and the marginalized (and rarely do).

The classic example is the issue of land reforms in India. The national and state governments passed progressive legislation in support of land reforms twenty years ago. Yet, very little of that has been implemented to date; largely because of the absence of "political will" resulting from the confluence of political and economic interests likely to be hurt if land reforms were implemented.

The current concern with the "absence of political will" is a clear example of the fact that the State need not necessarily act in common collective interest, which serves the "public good" for all. The State can serve some interest more than others and these are the powerful, organized political and economic interests which control it.

Civil Society

The notion of Civil Society needs to be introduced here. What is Civil Society? The references to the construct of Civil Society have varied in the theory of politics and governance (Bratton, 1991). Historically, Civil Society was the arena for organizing governance, material activities, and intellectual, moral and cultural aspects of communities. However, with the presence of the modern State, (in whatever form) in the contemporary context, it is difficult to understand Civil Society without a simultaneous reference to the State. Bratton (1991) describes the State-Civil Society dynamic in the contemporary context as a Ying-Yang metaphor. Viewed in such a way, and following the Gramscian perspective, the State can be seen to represent the "politics of domination," as Civil Society represents the "politics of consent." Thus, the State and Civil Society are both simultaneously needed to complete the process of governance of society. The State represents the structures of governance and Civil Society creates the values and normative framework for governance.

Society is thus comprised of three elements (Bratton, 1991): (a) material base of resources for productive utilization; (b) institutional base of associations, groups, and initiatives for conducting the affairs of Civil Society; and (c) ideological base of values, norms and ideals that provide the legitimacy for governance. Thus, institutions of Civil Society — family, clan, community, neighborhood associations, productive enterprises, service mechanisms — historically utilized the material resources of Civil Society in pursuit of its ideals and values.

The dominance of the State has significantly stripped the material base of Civil Society. In some instances, the State has taken over the material base (like all land, forest and water is State "property"); in some others, it has facilitated the growth of concentration of ownership of and control over the material base in a few private hands. As discussed earlier, the State has, with destruction of the material base of Civil Society, also destroyed or delegitimized the institutional base of Civil Society. And the State has continuously attempted to appropriate the ideological base from Civil Society. As "alien" State, its public functions in many countries of the South did not become rooted in the moral and ideological base of Civil Society, but remained cut-off or disconnected from it. The Gramscian notion of "hegemony" is rooted in Civil Society. Yet, the State and the ruling elites, attempt to control the intellectual base of Civil Society, along with its material base in order to perpetuate their hegemony over Civil Society. In Western capitalist societies, such ideological hegemony of the State and existing ruling order is attempted to be established through private mechanisms of media, education and culture. The single party Marxist States attempted it through public institutions and propaganda. The countries of the South seem to be using a combination of both (State control over TV/Radio and privatised education, for example). It is this process which constricts citizenship and restricts the participation of people in governance of their communities and lives. The State and its ruling/controlling elites become supreme; Civil Society becomes subservient to, dominated and ruled by the State and ruling elites.

New Relationship

Recent events in Eastern Europe, developments in Ethiopia (and much of Africa), new democratic governments in Latin America and associations for democratic space in several countries of Asia, are reflections of the pressures towards the need for renegotiating the balance of relationship between the State and Civil Society.

In various studies of democracy across the world, it has been documented again and again, that the greatest threat to democratic functioning has been the dominance of the State over the institutions of Civil Society (Diamond et. al. 1989). Wherever democracy has been threatened or derailed, wherever fascist and authoritarian tendencies (including military dictatorship) have taken over, it has been a consequence of the "supremacy" of the State over Civil Society and the dismantling of the institutions of Civil Society built over a period of history. Seen in this context, therefore, the relationship between the State and Civil Society needs to be reformulated.

The foregoing analysis tends to suggest three significant ways in which this relationship needs to be re-formulated.

Accountability

The State and its agencies, institutions and structures need to be accountable to Civil Society. This has several implications. The accountability implies rootedness of the State, its institutions and practices, in the culture, morality, values and norms of Civil Society. Alien forms of State apparatus and practices, policies and programs, will result in weakening these roots. Alien models of governance will ensure continued absence of accountability. The capabilities of Civil Society, its institutions and actors need to match the requirements of governance if that rootedness and accountability has to be ensured.

The second dimension of this accountability are the mechanisms of critiquing, questioning, debating and rejecting policies, programs, approaches and decisions of the State, its agencies, agents, and officials.

Civil Society is "supreme", not the State. Thus any rules, policies and procedures that the State construes need to be examined by Civil Society. In order for Civil Society to develop informed opinion and build a public judgement on it, it needs to have access to information; the process of formulating those policies, laws, rules and procedures needs to be an open and public process; and mechanisms for arriving at public judgement need to be strengthened.

In both these respects of *ensuring accountability of the State to Civil Society,* the institutions of Civil Society are critical. It is in this sense that NGO's, voluntary associations, citizens initiatives, neighborhood groups, all become critical in ensuring that the State becomes accountable to Civil Society, and not vice-versa.

Mediation

It is important to recognize that the State represents macro, aggregated, cumulated formations and structures in a country. As a result, State policies, agencies, officials operate at a level far more macro than the level of the family.

The relation between the State, its agencies and officials and that of the family needs to be *mediated* in a manner that maintains the balance between the State and Civil Society. The contemporary reality is that the State is so powerful, so controlling, so mighty in the face of an individual family, that it can do anything it likes and get away with that. For the power balancing between the family and the State to occur, mediating institutions are needed in Civil Society.

Studies have indicated that neighborhood associations, churches, voluntary organizations etc., have acted as mediating structures between the individual family and government institutions (Burger and Neuhans, 1977). It is in this sense that State power which tends to be totalitarian and coercive can be balanced with mediating institutions of Civil Society. NGOs, voluntary development organizations, and community associations thus become the institutions of Civil Society, ensuring this mediation between the family and the State; and ensuring the balance of power between the totalitarian tendencies of State power with the countervailing power of Civil Society.

Public

For a balanced relationship between the State and Civil Society, it is necessary to *redefine the meaning of the public and the private.* Current conceptualizations have resulted in a definition that equates "private" with what goes on inside a family (more so within a nuclear family) and "public" with what concerns the government. Thus there is *no space* left for Civil Society. The space is either private for the family; or the space is public — for the government. We need to re-formulate our understanding of what is public and what is private.

First, it is important to recognize that everything that is private is not necessarily left to the whims and fancies of individual families. Private opinions become the basis for evolving a public position and the question of privacy is a relative issue within the broader frame-work of a community. The norms, practices, values, preferences of

Civil Society provide the backdrop in which privacy and private arena within the family are defined.

Similarly, everything that is of public interest, everthing that is of interest beyond private, everything that concerns the public arena and public good, does not automatically become a concern for the State or its agencies. In fact, Civil Society itself is a public formulation. Before the rise of the modern State, institutions of Civil Society governed the "public arena."

So everything that is of public interest, everything that requires public concern, everything that requires public intervention need not be defined, controlled or monopolized by the State or its agencies (Burger and Neuhans, 1977). By recognizing that "public" concerns Civil Society, the State can create enabling mechanisms and conditions for Civil Society to "manage" public affairs within communities. This will ensure pluralism; this will ensure a particular response to particular needs and situations (as opposed to uniform and homogenous strategies to diverse conditions and situations). This will ensure that local needs, aspirations, requirements, conditions can influence local solutions, approaches and practices. This is the meaning of pluralism; this is the meaning of particular and specific response as opposed to uniform or homogenous strategy. This is the essential meaning of democracy.

Democratic institutions essentially imply institutions of Civil Society, which are capable of governing public concerns, without dependence on, or abdication to, the State and its agencies. It is in this sense that the State needs to "pull back." It does not mean that the State provision of services in health, education, etc. should be completely dismantled. It means that the State responsibility for the provision of those services needs to be re-defined. The State's responsibility is not necessarily to render those services on its own, but to foster conditions and mechanisms that are conducive to enabling to the institutions of Civil Society to meet the specific needs of their communities. The State becomes an enabler, and *not* a provider. The institutions of Civil Society are strengthened to ensure provision of services.

This does not imply de-centralization, because de-centralization then means that institutions of the government and the State continue to play similar roles at the local level as well. This implies a re-definition of the "public" — all that is public need not be the exclusive preserve of the government. In fact, it is Civil Society which should be responsible for governing public arenas, with the State playing enabling and supporting roles. It is in this sense that voluntary institutions, NGOs, neighborhood groups and citizen initiatives need to strengthen the capacities of Civil Society to govern the public arena.

Implications for NGOs

The foregoing analysis suggests several implications for NGOs and other voluntary associations and groups. In this section, implications for the roles and functions of development NGOs (and voluntary development organizations) are explored more specifically.

Conceptual

The reformulation of Civil Society-State relationship puts primacy on strengthening Civil Society. NGOs are one set of institutions within Civil Society. They are, therefore, part of the public domain of governance by Civil Society. This implies that *NGOs need to be seen as public institutions,* of Civil Society, engaged in the process of strengthening Civil Society in its relationship vis-a-vis the State and the ruling elites.

This conceptualization then challenges the growing trend of equating voluntary development NGOs with the private sector (the World Bank, Reagan-Bush-Thatcher "isms" all look at NGOs as part of the private sector). It questions the American label of NGOs as PVOs ("Private Voluntary Organizations"). It further challenges the restrictive economic notion of NGOs as exemplified by labels like "non-profits." It explodes the myth of moral superiority of the State over NGOs as represented in the public-private dichotomy of Governmental and Non-Governmental. It opens up the question of political and ideological dimensions of NGOs, and not merely their techno-managerial capabilities (as propounded by many; see James, 1989). Conceptually, therefore, NGOs are located in Civil Society which is supreme vis-a-vis the State and the ruling elites. This can then clarify contemporary confusion related to the nature of the relationship between NGOs and Government, and between NGOs and the private sector.

Strategic

Strengthening Civil Society in contemporary context implies strengthening its material, institutional and ideological bases. It further implies new approaches to governance and politics. It implies strengthening "citizenship." The development NGOs can play strategic roles in this context through their programmes and activities. They can (as many do already) address the issue of recovering the material base of Civil Society through greater access to and control over the resources by the local communities and people's organizations. They can facilitate the process of generating informed public judgement and of becoming active citizenry. Interventions aimed at strengthening the capacity of its own, and other, institutions of Civil Society, to critique the existing development paradigm and to evolve an alternative people-centered, community-based, citizen-governed development paradigm can be useful in this regard. Facilitating increased citizen access to and engagement with public policy issues can help to alter the practice of governance.

The role of NGOs in strengthening Civil Society to regain and retain hegemony over the State and private enterprise is another critical strategic function. Challenging the continuous attempts to control the minds of people, expanding and systematizing popular knowledge, expanding social control over education and science, strengthening mechanisms for democratisation of knowledge, promoting philosophical and normative debate around issues of public concern, encouraging civic articulation of parameters of governance, facilitating promotion of ideas related to social distribution of power and accountability of the State to Civil Society, etc. are some of the

strategic roles that development NGOs can (and sometimes do) play in support of strengthening the ideological base of Civil Society. Civil Society needs to be enabled to articulate its framework and values of unity within diversity - a task that NGOs can facilitate. NGOs can strengthen the practice of citizenship by encouraging the people to view themselves as producers of culture, ideas and values.

Another strategic consideration in this context is the need for strengthening international linkages across civil societies - an "international Civil Society." This becomes particularly important in light of growing international connectedness between private capital (as clearly represented by multinationals) and State apparatus (as in many regional and global structures of intergovernmental institutions). In the contemporary context, the issue of governance and hegemony has international dimensions as well. The challenge to the power of multinational corporations and "the new world (governmental) order" (as explained by President Bush of U.S.A.) necessitates strengthening international linkages across Civil Societies. Development NGOs, through their existing networks and associations, may now be strategically positioned to facilitate those linkages.

Institutional

The strengthening of the institutional base of Civil Society requires simultaneous emphasis on material and ideological bases. Yet, as contemporary manifestations of one set of institutions of Civil Society, development NGOs themselves need a stronger institutional base. The capacities for engaging in various programmes and activities suggested in the previous section need to be institutionalized in NGOs and other formations of Civil Society (PRIA, 1990). Instead of getting bogged down with the "supposedly" temporary and transitory nature of their existence, development NGOs need to strengthen their institutional capacities to perform the strategic roles described before.

This raises the question about the need for elaborating mechanisms for ensuring accountability of NGOs to Civil Society. It necessitates focusing current concern for NGO accountability away from governmental mechanisms to mechanisms governed by Civil Society. It also opens up issues related to the material base of NGO institutions themselves. Strategies to strengthen the presently fragile and weak material base of most development NGOs need to be evolved within this framework.

Finally, development NGOs can help strengthen (or rebuild) institutional mechanisms within Civil Society to provide for services to families and communities. As the State shifts its role from "provider" of services to "enabler," there is a risk towards "privatisation" of services (like education, healthcare, etc.). While resisting the current pressures for and temptations of becoming service-providers themselves, development NGOs can help contribute to the strengthening of institutional arrangements within Civil Society for "public" provision of such services.

The reformulation presented in this paper may seem to imply a "tall order" for development NGOs. Yet, the contemporary global reality makes demands on the community of development NGOs to work towards this challenge. The regional and national contexts vary considerably in terms of the relationship between Civil Society and the State, as well as the nature and strength of development NGOs. Therefore, specific strategies and their particular manifestation may vary considerably across countries and regions. Yet, it is an inescapable challenge!

Annex 2

ORGANIZATIONS OF CIVIL SOCIETY: BANGLADESH

- -

By Richard Holloway

Let us look at typology of organisations of civil society, which we have developed. As you see, a fundamental distinction if between those organisations operating for the benefit of their members, and those operating for the benefit of others. The Governance structure, the accountability, the access to resources, the links to outsiders all depend on whether the organisation is a creation of its members for itself, or a creation of individuals for others.

As in many attempts to develop typologies, and put everything relevant into boxes, there are certain things which do not fit, or which need to be further explained:

Membership Organisations (helping themselves)

Indigenous Organisations of the Community

Gusthi and Samaj are organisations that people are born into, and to some extent they do not reflect voluntarily chosen membership, but a person is always at liberty either to be active in such groupings, or let their "membership" slide and be inactive. Community clubs (for sports, welfare, culture, religion etc) on the other hand require a voluntary commitment.

Induced Community Groups

Here outsiders (individual, the Government, maybe political parties) have suggested some form of association to community members, and they have freely decided to join because they can see some personal advantage in doing so. Often to be part of what is generally considered "Development", people have joined (for instance) mothers' clubs in order to help each other and access services from others, associations of those receiving water from one irrigation source, associations of family planning acceptors, parent teacher associations for management of local schools etc.

Mass Organisations

Many mass organisations have their origins in political parties which developed mass membership organisations in order to further the political party's mobilisation of votes for gaining political power. Many mass organisations have, however, grown beyond their close affiliation to political parties, and are now mass organisations which include people of a variety of political shadings, or none at all. Cultural organisations like Samiliti Sangskritik Jote, womens organisations like Bangladesh Mohila Samity, peasant organisations like Bangladesh Khet Mohila Samity, peasant organisations like Bangladesh Khet Majur Samity have all evolved from partisan political affiliation.

The noteworthy exception is mass organisations of youth which, in nearly all cases, have been and continue to be controlled, by political parties. At the time of the overthrow of Ershad, student organisations seemed to have climbed out of the bog of party politics, but they have sunk back again.

Cooperatives

In theory cooperatives are pre-eminently organisations of civil society — associations of people with a common interest and common economic background. In fact the Government in Bangladesh, and in many other countries, has appointed a Registrar of Cooperatives whose function is to make sure that the coopreatives keep to the rules of cooperative law, and keep honest. This puts cooperatives

into a hazy category where they are partly induced community groups (induced by the Government) and partly Government organisations. There are, however, a sizeable number of very much more independent cooperatives started privately, (not started by the Government) and merely registered with the Government, of which the best example is Deedar Cooperative in Comilla.

Religious Societies

In nearly every village of Bangladesh there is a mosque, and there is usually a mosque committee to manage it and to manage other activities carried out by the *imam*. In other cases there are prayer groups and occasionally *tabliq* or religious conventions. These are often linked to the activities of *pir* - religious leaders who have a larger audience and group of devotees than the *imam* of a single mosque.

What is true of members of Islam is also largely true, in a much smaller way, of members of Hinduism, Buddhism and Christianity.

Trade Organisations

These can usefully be divided into those organisations which bring the employees together, like Trade Unions: those which bring the employers together, like Chambers of Commerce or Business Associations, and those which bring the self-employed together (like weavers or fishermen in areas where their trade is practised). One anomaly in Bangladesh is that Trade Unions are all modern sector industrial workers organisations — there are no Trade Unions of agricultural workers or peasants.

Professional Associations

The professions, like Journalists, Lawyers, Engineers, Primary Teachers, have all got their own "trade unions" to look after their interests. In some cases these associations overlap with mass organisations e.g. students, and in some cases, as with mass organisations, they have become involved with partisan politics.

Non-Membershp Organisations (helping others)

Local Institutions

In many cases local landed families have set up schools or madrassahs for the the benefit of local people. In many cases they have ensured the sustainability of these institutions by making a *waqf* endowment of land or pond to these local institutions. In some cases (like the Eskander Foundation) such individuals have formalised their philanthropy in an organisation and there are also a few business houses which have set up trusts and foundations.

NGOs

NGOs are only one part of civil society, though in common usage the word "NGO" is often used to refer to all sorts of other part of civil society. It is surprising that Bangla has taken over the English word "NGO" without translation, although Bangla is rich in associated words like sangstha, samity, sangothon etc. "NGO" is a very imprecise word which is used in many different ways usually depending on the perspective of the user.

Of course, primarily and fundamentally "NGO", by definition means an organisation which is not part of the Government, but this definition is so imprecise as to be useless since this also includes the business sector.

Secondly it is often used as meaning the same as "voluntary organisation" (in which case it would overlap with all of the membership organisations listed above). A more precise and useful definition is "a non-membership organisation formed for providing welfare and development services to the poor" — and this immediately sub-divides into Welfare Organisations and Socio-Economic Development Organisations.

A third commonly used definition is often colloquially expressed as "organisations like BRAC and Proshika" which really means non-membership socio-economic development organisations, often using foreign funds. Such organisations in a recent meeting expressed their disatisfaction with the unclear label "NGO" and decided to canvas its members to change themselves into Private Voluntary Develoment Organisations (PVDOs). NGOs in this sense break out into the following sub-categories:

Implementing Organisations

Organisations which take a direct role of implementing development programs for the poor, usually through working with groups they help to form, and which they call "Peoples Organisations".

Peoples Organisations

These are the groups which the NGOs have helped to form. They overlap completely with induced community groups listed above at A2, and can overlap with mass organisations. Both Khet Majur Samity and Mohila Parishad are registered as NGOs.

Support Organisations

These are NGOs which help other NGOs to improve their implementation of projects through training, technical assistance, research, lobbying etc.

Networks and Forums

These are groupings of NGOs around a particular issue or sector.

Apex Organisations

These are the representative organisations for the NGO sector. In the case of the development NGOs, the Apex Organisation is ADAB.

Area-Based Benevolent Societies

In Dhaka there are many *samity* which represent the native sons and daughters of different regions of Bangladesh, and which take responsibility for looking after the interest of people from that locale. A very interesting spin on this is that such *samity* often mobilise native sons and daughters who have left Bangladesh and are living overseas.

Service Clubs

These clubs, like Rotary, Lions, Soroptomists etc. which are all based on foreign models, and usually affiliated to them, are joined by a few local clubs inherited from colonial days (Dhaka Club, Narayangani Club etc). Their main motive is as social clubs for the elites, but they often mobilise funds for welfare and development activities, and sometimes become implementing organisations themselves (like Lions' Eye Camps).

Non-Profit Companies

This category is hazy at the edges. It encompasses organisation which are often similar in concept to developmental NGOs (i.e. Private Voluntary Development Organisations) but which are also non-profit businesses. Examples are the Polli Kormo Shahayak Foundation, the Social Marketing Company, MIDAS, and the Grameen Bank. Grameen Bank, however, is a membership organisation and is growing large enough to be thought of as a mass organisation.

Spurious Organisations (not helping)

As with all legitimate activities of society, we would be surprised if we did not find some examples of a black or spurious side to civil society. Just as there are illegitimate Governments and Businesses, there are also illegitimate organisation of civil society.

There are:

Come 'N GOs

This witty name represents those organisations set up by unscrupulous individuals for personal profit, but represented by them as private, voluntary organisations for the common good. Their activities usually last as long as the campaign to raise funds, at which time the organiser decamps with the money.

GONGOs

This is Government organised NGOs where Government, seeing advantages of carrying out its activities under the banner of an

NGO, disguises a government activity as an NGO. They are neither private nor voluntary, but controlled by Government — a good example in Bangladesh was the Patuakhali Trust.

DONGOs

These are Donor-organised NGOs. Donor organisations are sometimes so enthusiastic to push their particular policy or implement their own programs that they set up front NGOs which are in fact controlled by the Donors.

BONGOs

These are Business-organised NGOs. Business houses may very well and very legitimately set up independent foundations, but in some cases businesses will set up NGOs simply in order to acquire advantages from tax breaks or specific imports.

❦

Annex 3

THAI NGOS AND CIVIL SOCIETY

- -

By Gawin Chutima

In Thailand, the October 14 event in 1973 marks a place in Thai history for changing the relationship between the state and the people. It was for the first time that civil society could play any role in Thai politics.

Immediately after that October day, it was a time of "blossoming democracy", when after more than a decade under military dictatorship, Thai people came out to demand their freedom, justice and better life. However, this was a short period and the young generation whose enthusiasm for new-found freedom found expression in many activities was crushed by the right-wings and another military coup d'etat, and for three years after October 6, 1976, intellectual and personal freedom died. A large number of intellectuals joined the Communist Party of Thailand (CPT) and its armed struggle against the government. But gradually, the government suppression relaxed and disillusioned political exiles trickled back from the jungles. Then the CPT collapsed.

This period coincided with the expansion of another movement, which throughout the political and social turmoil, had been

This paper was prepared for the Thai delegation from NGO-CORD to the General Assembly of El Taller in Tunis, Tunisia, during 21-25 October, 1993.

Gawin Chutima is now a consultant for NGOs in project formulation, reporting, monitoring and evaluation. He used for work as a National Coordinator for NGO-CORD from January 1991 to April 1993.

content to move slowly and scrupulously to effect social change. Since then the movement which is now known as non-governmental organizations, or NGOs, has established itself as a powerful voice of conscience in Thai society, or in other words, a major group in Thai civil society.

There is not a common agreement, even among NGO workers themselves, about the link between the historic event of 20 years ago and NGO movement of today. Certainly, there are NGO workers who used to be student activists in the mid 70s, then joined the CPT in late 70s and returned to work for NGOs. Many people who are NGO leaders now may not be in NGOs if the event did not take place as they were exposed to the masses, including workers and peasants, drew their interest to politics, and learned about social conscience through activities that sprang up after the event. Fundamentally, the desire for social justice and people's power are also the basis of both the student movement and NGO movement. This leads a number of NGO workers to believe that the NGOs and October 14 are the same movement.

However, number of people who swelled the NGOs' ranks included not only those who returned from the jungles after the insurgency ended, but also those who did not flee to the jungles but who still held on their desire for social justice. Another argument against the link was that although the event has played an important role in shaping the mass movement in the past twenty years, the mass movement which was the result of the event was leaning to socialism where taking over of state power by force if necessary, was the only way to achieve any meaningful change, while the NGO movement is non-violent and anti-centralisation.

It may be then not correct to say that October 14 event was a direct inspiration for the growth of NGOs. But the event can also be considered to shape the philosophy and give strength to the NGO movement. Thirayuth Boonmi, a former student leader whose arrest with 12 other people for publicly demanding a constitution sparked the student movement that led to the October 14 uprising, says that when socialism proved not to be the answer, many people looked for another way out; that was when the NGO movement received a big boost.

As in other countries, those who were young middle class people in Thailand went through the age of soul-searching and were shaped by their direct experience, learning by trial and error in political events. In the end, a number of these relatively highly-educated people or intellegentsia who still felt that they wanted to do something to change social injustice that still prevailed and refused to enter political parties which they saw was no hope chose to join the weak non-profit organizations to work within the system and yet were free enough to pursue their vision, infusing it with youthful and idealistic energy. The 1980s after the collapse of CPT was then a renaissance for non-profit organizations which subsequently became known as NGOs and began to resemble a social movement.

Actually, groups with social concerns existed before October 14 event, but were not known as NGOs. They were rather non-profit organizations, concentrating mainly on social welfare, cultural identity or literacy issues. Only later did they branch out to other areas, such as rural poverty. To be precise, only after the October 14 event did organizations concerned with democratic and human rights appear. Organizations concerned with environment even came later only in the last ten years. In the 1960s and 1970s, therefore, as Thirayuth comments, the NGOs were mere non-profit groups, not a movement at all, and certainly not the NGOs as they are today. This is confirmed by Dej Phumkhacha, a veteran NGO worker, who says that NGOs today are much different from what they were; a lot has been learned since October 14 and much improvement have been made to raise the level of NGOs, including their quality and strategy of development.

Banthorn Ondam, an academic and another veteran NGO worker, points low profile. Starting only in about 1987 that NGOs became more active as the country's industrial develoment got into high gear, creating a "crisis of natural resources and environment." This was the time when NGOs working in political and human rights and those in the developmental field began cooperating more, and NGOs working on the same issues or with the same target groups joined into networks for policy advocacy. At the same time, NGOs became more active and clearer in assisting the people to organize themselves to solve problems they faced by themselves. In this process, the NGOs reached out to get supports from sympathetic people mainly among the academics and media people, but also included few government officials. Alliance building had become another strategy of the NGOs even if they did not understand it quite well. All these progress contributed to the more visible presentation of Thai NGOs in national arena as "the voice of conscience" fighting for justice on behalf of the people, and they were named "People of the Year" by a leading political magazine at the end of 1990.

However, the hope for participatory democracy was crushed in February 1991 when the military took over in a coup d'etat which ended twelve consecutive years of relative freedom. For a while, NGOs kept low profile, but they gradually reasserted themselves step by step, becoming the first group to openly denounce and act in opposition to the coup. They built up vast networks of people against the military which tried to remain in control of the government even after an election in March 1992 and eventually led the May 17-20 democracy demonstrations, which led to the downfall of the military-led government. Since then, the movement has become an even more infuential voice in the nation's political and economic development.

They made several steps forwards into shaping the system during the Anand interim government, as never happened before. Paradoxically, many of these inroads were taken aback in the elected government of Prime Minister Chuan Leekpai whose five-party coalition came to power on the bill of democracy. This government was also the first one which came out to publicly and systematically attack NGOs which have been increasingly disillusioned and began to criticize it. The charge is actually an old one propped up again and again throughout the movement's history; NGOs exaggerate problems in order to get funded by foreign sources and then become a tool or front of foreign powers to undermine national security or strength.

Under this attack, what are relationships between NGOs and the middle class? It seems that the middle class played important roles in the May event and NGOs have realised that they have to build alliances with them. However, the relationships are in fact not that smooth and some times even abrasive.

It is no doubt that the people in NGOs come from the middle class and NGOs owe their fundamental strength to the student and intellectual movement of middle class people. However, the movement by and large serves the majority of people at the lower level. A conflict of economic interests happens. On the one hand, many problems faced by the people are caused by the middle class's consumer lifestyle and capitalist mode of production. Witoon Permpongsacharoen, a leading environmentalist/NGO worker points out that the middle class lags behind NGOs. Environmental problems, for instance, are an issue of conscience of middle class in post-industrial countries, but Thai middle class has not gotten that far yet, they are still thinking about the stock market and economic development in a way that is out-of-date in the capitalist world at large.

On the other hand, the middle class ignores NGOs as they are more concerned with supporting political or business groups that they could gain something. They have no hope of gaining from a relationship with NGOs as NGOs do not identify with any political or business interest groups, and in many occasions, they even find NGOs opposing their interests.

However, as mentioned earlier, NGOs have begun to build bridges with the middle class, may be not so much with those in business but mainly with professionals such as lawyers, teachers and media people. They have definitely made inroads in this direction. But as the middle class is growing fast, NGOs have not yet demonstrated that they are able to serve or represent the middle class too even in the long term. The NGOs will have to adjust and will increase their role in this regard in the future. NGO leaders and some academics/social thinkers, such as Thirayuth and Dr. Kasian Techapira from Thammasat University, believe that the middle class will also work with NGOs increasingly because problems will affect them. Dr. Kasian, in particular, points out that it is in the interest of the state to separate the middle class from NGOs. They realise that when NGOs and the middle class cooperate, they make a great alliance as can be clearly seen from the May Event. If the state succeeds in hurting the NGOs, the middle class will feel pain the most.

The same as Dr. Kasian, Dr. Prawase Wasi, a leading academic and NGO worker, points out that possibility of violence at times will be great as Thailand is in a situation in which urban people are taking natural resources from rural people and the society lacks mechanism to prevent it. In his presentation on the *Balanced(-Power) Society in August* 1993, he proposes that instead of confronting the state and business sector which are so powerful and NGOs are hopeless to win over them, the NGOs should concentrate on positively strengthening the third sector, that is the people sector, until it is as strong as the other two sectors in order to create a balanced-power society. Development will be most effective and beneficial when all parties, at least five - the people and their organizations, NGOs, academics, media and government officials - join hands in the spirit of love and compassion, total alliance building in another name.

In the book *Civil Society* which is a collection of his articles in Thai press, Thirayuth Boonmi has pointed the importance of the "third power" as the only hope to solve the country problems since 1991. He indicates that this independent and creative third power will consist of "people who try to work as volunteer groups to serve the people in varous fields, such as religious groups, child welfare groups, women's groups or groups that work on conceptual level, culture or with political parties". Obviously, even though he does not use the word NGOs, the groups he mentions can not be anything else. However, he also predicts that it will be a long time before these groups can become a real movement and the general public recognize the necessity of this power.

Thirayuth also quotes the theory of Strong State-Weak Society vs. Weak State-Strong Society, and Thailand is likely to develop to be a Moderate State-Moderate Society. He shares with Dr. Prawas that the country needs balanced development in order to avoid crisis, solve problems and become prosperous. However, he shares more with NGOs than Dr. Prawase that the third power still have to keep monitoring and criticizing the state and business, advocating decentralisation of power instead of only looking for cooperation as human beings, however much good elements they have, also have the vice elements as well.

A common suggestion to the Thai NGOs by their leaders and sympathisers/well-wishers is really a challenge: The NGOs can represent people at any level, of ideological stripe, if they can show that they have a clear vision of future and offer viable alternatives for all the people who can not find satisfactory answers from the government, political parties and business sectors.

W.A Callahan, the director of the Philosophy, Politics and Economics Programme at Rangsut University in Bangkok, points out that emerging as an alternative form of organization which is classless and participatory, the NGOs are called to unite and be the vanguard of the 1990s. However, at their best, NGOs are not vanguards but facilitators. NGOs do not lead people, but coordinate action. They are not after state power, but "people's power". Thus, NGOs guard against recreating the monster of centralised repression that they are contesting. Even though he believes that this does signify a seismic shift, Callahan cautions that whether it will be successful or not remains to be seen.

These points are all confirmed by many NGO leaders and other academics who recognize that NGOs are a movement of diversity, if they are to be a movement. They are too independent that no one can tell them what to do. Even though NGOs will definitely be a major force in building up civil society or grassroots participatory democracy, they may not become a single movement of their own at all as many NGO workers wish they should not be.

References

1. Banthorn Ondam, *The NGOs and Thai Democracy, in Sungsidh Piriyarangsan and Pasuk Phongpaichit (eds.), The Middle Class and Thai Democracy,* The Political Economy Centre, Faculty of

Economics, Chulalongkorn University and Friedrich Ebert Stiftung, Khon Nangsue Press, Bangkok, May 1993.

2. Callahan, William A., *Three seismic shifts from 1973 to 1993*, in the Sunday Post, October 10, 1993.

3. Prawase Wasi, *Balanced-Power Society and the Methods (to achieve it)*, Amarin Print, Bangkok, August 1993.

4. Thirayuth Boonmi, *Civil Society*, Mingmitr Press, Bangkok, October 1993.

5. *October Uprising and the Voice of Conscience*, Report of a roundtable discussion of NGO workers and academics at the Bangkok Post on October 4, 1993 in the Sunday Post, October 10, 1993.

6. *NGO movement — An Angel or a devil?*, Report of a roundtable discussion of NGO workers and academics at the Bangkok Post on October 4, 1993 in the Sunday Post, October 17, 1993.

Annex 4

ASIA-PACIFIC IN THE 1990S: A PHILIPPINE PERSPECTIVE

By The Forum for Philippine Alternatives
    Asia-Pacific Cluster Group

Summary

The Asia-Pacific region is today marked by an unstable combination of US military predominance and Japanese economic hegemony.

The process by which Japan has emerged as the region's economic superpower can be characterized as the regionalization of the Japanese economy, with the integration cum subordination of the weaker and smaller economies to Japanese core economy.

To check the economic hegemony of Japan and prevent it from remilitarizing, many Asia-Pacific governments have sought to prolong the US military presence in the region. This has coincided with the agenda of some sectors of the US government and US military, which see the worsening economic and technological conflict between the US and Japan spilling over into the political and economic arena. Thus, it is likely that the Cold War will be succeeded by a volatile and unstable era of balance-of-power politics.

The unique characteristic of the Philippines in the regional equation is that it is in danger of being marginalized from the capital,

Prepared for the FOPA International Conference by the following members of FOPA's Asia-Pacific Cluster Group: Walden Bello, Ria Pugeda, and Akiko Naono. Other members of the cluster, based in Japan, are Kevin Unchida, Liza Go, Lester Ruiz and Miyoko Oshima.

trade, and technology flows sweeping the rest of the region. Because of their perception of the limited prospects for developing the Philippine market owing to very skewed income distribution, the Japanese are reluctant to make a strategic commitment to the Philippines, preferring by far to focus on Vietnam.

A progressive Philippine agenda oriented toward the region must begin with this reality of accelerating marginalization. A reorientation of both progressive and popular consciousness away from the United States and toward the Asia-Pacific is vital. So is a revision of the traditional progressive attitude toward foreign, and specifically Japanese, capital flows. Under an appropriate foreign investment regime, some members of the group feel, foreign capital can help develop vital sectors of an economy, create jobs, and transfer much-needed technology to the Philippines.

Such a foreign investment regime will, however, be ineffective unless it is part of a larger, regionally coordinated effort to maximize the positive effects of Japanese and other foreign investments and radically minimize their possible negative impact. More broadly, the Philippines must participate in an effort to create an "Asia-Pacific Technoeconomic Bloc" that would regulate the activities of Japanese capital while promoting coordinated efforts to increase the region's economic and technological independence vis-a-vis Japan.

Alongside the creation of an Asia-Pacific Technoeconomic Bloc must be the establishment of an Alternative Regional Security System that would promote long-term stability in the region by checking the US' tendency to unilaterally deploy force, moving conflicts from resolution by force to resolution by diplomacy, and pushing the region toward total denuclearization and significant demilitarization.

Finally, a progressive Philippine agenda for the region must include supporting the establishment of a Regional Congress of Non-Governmental and Popular Organizations that would bring the collective power of the region's NGOs to bear on those issues that both governments and foreign powers are either hostile or indifferent to, such as human rights, democratic rights, women's rights, minority rights, and the environment.

Introduction

Even before the end of the Cold War, the Asia-Pacific region had been substantially transformed from what it was at the height of US hegemony in the late 1960s and early 1970s.

During the latter period, the US was both militarily supreme and economically dominant. The US then deployed more than a million military personnel in the region. 500,000 of these troops were in Vietnam, and the rest were stationed in 300 bases or in the massive floating naval base that was the US Seventh Fleet. At the same time, huge capital outflows from the US in search of cheap labor in Asian sites like Singapore, South Korea, Taiwan, Malaysia, and the Philippines made the American corporations the dominant players in the regional economy.

Military in Search of a Mission

Today, the US remains dominant militarily but no longer hegemonic. Its last remaining foothold on the Asian mainland consists of 44,000 troops on the Korean peninsula. It has lost its bases in Vietnam, Thailand, and the Philippines. More important, the military forces of its allies have grown substantially, both in firepower and in numbers. Not counting submarines, for instance, Japan now has the biggest surface fleet in the Western Pacific, one that is larger than the formidable Seventh Fleet.

The US military presence remains impressive in scale, but it is on the verge of an institutional crisis induced by the sudden loss of its traditional mission of containing communism. With the end of the Cold War, the US military in the Pacific is in search for a new mission, one which would convince an increasingly budget-conscious Congress to continue releasing the $60 billion needed annually to sustain its high-level military profile in the area. The definition of the US military's post-Cold War in the Pacific mission has become particularly urgent to many US policymakers, who are upset at the realization that it was under a canopy of US military power that Japanese corporations marginalized US business and established their economic hegemony in the region.

The Japanese Ascendancy

Japan is now indisputably the region's hegemonic economic power, as is evident from the following indicators:

❖ Between 1950 and 1991, Japan invested a total of $74.8 billion in the region, in contrast to US investment of $43.6 billion. Over 70 per cent of the total Japanese investments — some $53 billion — came in between 1985 and 1991.

In 1990 alone, the Japanese invested a total of $6.6 billion in Malaysia, Indonesia, Thailand, Vietnam, China, and the Philippines, or nearly twice the US investment of $3.5 billion. While much of the Japanese investments went into new projects, most of the American investments went mainly to maintaining existing operations. Asian business circles, in fact, now talk about the "disappearing European and US investors."

❖ Japan is now the region's most important trading partner. While the US is still ahead of Japan as an import absorber, it has now consolidated its position as the top exporter to the region, enjoying a trade surplus with practically all its neighboring economies.

❖ Japan is now the area's main source of technology, particularly high technology; in the late 1980s, the value of Japan's exports of high technology to the East Asian and Southeast Asian economies was twice that of the United States.

❖ Japan is the principal source of bilateral aid to the region, providing more than twice the US level. Between 1985 and 1989, over half of Japan's official development aid of $25 billion went to the Asia-Pacific region. It must be noted, however, that only 50 per cent of this aid was in the form of grants, the rest being loans that have to be repaid.

The massive inflow of Japanese capital was the main source of the explosive growth rates in the 1980s of the Southeast Asian economies, with the important exception of the Philippines. More importantly, this growth was accompanied by the increasing integration of the different national economies around the Japanese economy.

The Japanese Economy and the NICs

This process of integration cum subordination is best seen in the case of the two paramount NICs ("newly industrializing countries"), Korea and Taiwan. While the two economies are often seen as present or potential rivals to Japan, the relationship is one of structural dependence or integration into the core, Japanese economy. Whereas Taiwan and Korea are often portrayed as developing integrated economies, with growing high-tech sectors, the fact of the matter is that neither has been able to graduate from being essentially labor-intensive assembly sites for foreign and specifically Japanese components. Indeed, nearly 30 years after initiating export-oriented industrialization, Taiwan and Korea are now even more dependent technologically on Japan. This is revealed most dramatically by the two countries' $8 billion + trade deficits with Japan, which do not reflect evanescent trade movements but a fundamental technological dependency.

Taiwan's microchip industry is so dependent on Japanese semiconductor-manufacturing equipment that, in the words of one Taiwanese industry specialist, "If the Japanese refuse to sell the equipment, you're lost." As for Korea, its image of being a high-tech producer is belied by a few sobering realities; the bestselling Hyundai Excel may be Korea's best-known export, but its body styling is Italian in origin, its engine is designed by the Japanese firm Mitsubishi, and its transmission is both designed and manufactured by Mitsubishi. Korean television sets may be competing toe-to-toe with Japanese products in the US, but Japanese components account for 85 per cent of their value. Korea may be the world's fifth largest exporter of computers, but only the computer cabinet, confesses one of the country's leading electronics journals, is actually made in the country.

In the 1980s, Japanese corporations moved to more systematically exploit the structural dependence of the NICs by integrating them as subordinate elements within an Asia-Pacific-wide division of labor designed to enhance their profitability. In the automobile industry, for instance, Mitsubishi bought a 15 per cent stake in Hyundai Motors, and it has integrated the Korean carmaker into its system of international production by having it produce key parts of selected Mitsubishi models like the "Debonair" or "Montero." Practically all Taiwanese carmakers now have significant Japanese equity investments, and they have been reoriented into a regional division of labor which one Japanese analyst describes as "not an equal division of labor as seen in the European countries, but a vertical one within the automobile industry as a whole." In this "inter-product division of labor," the Taiwanese firms specialize in "low-price compact cars which have fewer parts and a higher percentage of labor in the entire process." Perhaps unwittingly using historically loaded terms, the writer concludes that Taiwan "aims for coexistence and coprosperity with Japan by producing those items that are not economically suitable for Japan [to produce]."

The Japanese Economy and Southeast Asia

The explosion of Japanese investment in Southeast Asia that occurred in the mid-eighties — when the sharp rise in the value of the yen relative to the dollar forced the Japanese to look for low-cost manufacturing sites outside Japan — was more consciously geared at integration of the region around the needs of the Japanese core economy than the earlier Japanese penetration of Korea and Taiwan. Investment is planned from a regional perspective to take maximum advantage of "differing labor costs, consumption patterns, regulations, and locational advantage in manufacturing."

In the case of Matsushita, for instance, each country is assigned specific items to produce for export: color TVs and electric irons in Malaysia, semiconductors in Singapore, and dry-cell batteries, floppy disk drives, and electronic capacitors in the Philippines. Likewise, car companies like Nissan, Toyota, and Mitsubishi have worked out regional specialization schemes. In the Toyota scheme, Indonesia specializes in gasoline engines and stamped parts, Malaysia turns out steering links and electrical equipment, the Philippines produces transmissions, and Thailand manufactures diesel engines, along with stamped parts and electrical equipment. Toyota then assembles the whole car in Thailand and ships the completed product to Japan or the United States.

Along with this horizontal integration of Japanese corporate subsidiaries located in different countries, a process of vertical integration is tightening the links of the region to the core economy. The first phase of this process, which began in the mid-1980s, saw automobile and consumer electronics firms relocate their plants from Japan to the region. This was followed by the outmigration of smaller companies supplying parts and components for the auto and electronics manufacturers. A third phase of backward integration may be about to begin, with the relocation of heavy and chemical industries providing basic inputs to both the big manufacturers and their suppliers.

Regionalization of the Japanese Economy

These processes of corporate-driven horizontal and vertical integration underline the fact that what has occurred in the last few years has been less the creation of a regional economy with plural centers but the regionalization of Japanese industry. This geographical dispersal of the different components of Japanese industry is, in turn, one dimension of a broader process of functional economic integration that is hierarchical in character rather than reciprocal, with Southeast Asia, Vietnam, and China specializing in the provision of cheap labor for manufacturing; Southeast Asia, Australia, the Russian Far East and China serving as a source for raw materials and commodities; and the mature NICs — Taiwan, Korea, Singapore, and Hong Kong — as well as Australia serving as a site for selected less-than-state of the art high-tech industries as well as middle-class markets.

And at the center of this universe lies Japan, which will soon displace the United States as the main market for the region's manufactures and resources, and which now serves as the main destination of profits, the source of capital, and the creator and dispenser of high technology.

In short, debate on whether there will be an Asia-Pacific trading bloc that will emerge to counter the North American Free Trade Area or the European Community is, as one observer puts it, "somewhat immaterial because a de facto trading bloc is already emerging. It is arising out of economic necessity and, barring draconian barriers, will continue to grow regardless of whether or not free trade among the various economies develop. Japan's executives do not need free trade to operate."

The Dynamics of Unequal Exchange

This process of dependent integration into the Japanese core economy is inherently unstable and conflictive. One of the main sources of instability is Japan's tendency to export more than its imports — a tendency that is very pronounced with respect to the NICs, and increasingly the case with the newer industrializing economies, like Thailand and Malaysia, as Japanese subsidiaries increase their imports of expensive, sophisticated high-tech equipment from their mother industries in Japan. Unequal exchange or the net flow of wealth to the region's center from the periphery and semi-periphery is the key structural feature of the economic relationship of Japan to the Asia-Pacific. This is principally a reflection of Japan's monopolization of advanced technology, which allows it to add significantly more value to its products relative to the low-tech manufactured products, processed agricultural products, and raw materials that it imports from the dependent Asia-Pacific economies.

The Philippines in the Asia-Pacific Division of Labor

Where, specifically, does the Philippines fit in this Japanese-dominated division of labor?

Without ascribing a judgment as to whether Japanese-investment growth is good or bad, the fact of the matter is that while neighboring economies are booming as a consequence of the massive entry of Japanese capital, the reality is that the Philippines is being relegated to a marginal status in the regional economy. This may not seem evident from national investment figures. These figures show that Japan outstripped the United States as the top foreign investor in 1989 and 1990, and its cumulative stock of investment in the country of $1.8 billion has now topped the $1.7 that the US has invested here. However, looked at comparatively, as a recipient of Japanese foreign investment, the Philippines received the least amount of all major Asia-Pacific economies between 1950 and 1991. The $1.7 billion invested in the Philippines was puny, compared to $7.7 billion for tiny Singapore, $4.4 billion for Korea, and almost $12.7 billion for Indonesia.

While it is true that significant amounts of Taiwanese and Hong kong capital have been coming in recent years, these are usually short-term, speculative capital meant to turn a quick profit in commercial or speculative operations before just as quickly leaving the country. Japanese investment, on the other hand, is often long-term in outlook and represent a long-term commitment to an economy. And what the comparative investment figures indicate is that the Japanese are indeed quite reluctant to make a long-term economic commitment to the Philippines.

A series of interviews that some members of the Asia-Pacific Cluster Group did in the summer of 1992 with key Filipino business people who are closely connected to Japanese firms confirmed that there is indeed strong hesitation on the part of the Japanese to commit significant capital to the Philippines, and that they are much more excited in investing in Vietnam than the Philippines. While law-and-order problems and foreign investment restrictions were cited as reasons, many respondents recognized that in other parts of the world, the Japanese can accommodate their operations to any law-and-order situation and foreign investment regime so long as markets are seen as expanding and profitable.

Probably a major reason for Japanese reluctance is the widespread perception that the Philippine market is quite small — that is, people with effective purchasing power are a relatively small part of the population. Japanese business, according to some respondents, is put off by the highly skewed distribution of income in the Philippines, which they see as the principal cause of economic stagnation. This hypothesis certainly needs more investigation. Nevertheless, it would be surprising if the Japanese foreign policy and corporate elite did not operate with an awareness of the fact that the dynamic markets in Korea, Taiwan, and Japan itself were originally created by social reform, specifically radical land reform, which created a distribution of wealth and income that was much less unequal in these societies than in other parts of the Third World. Aside from possessing a diligent and skilled labor force, Vietnam is likely to be much more attractive as the next "frontier" for Japanese investment than the Philippines, precisely for this very reason: that its relatively equitable distribution of income now will serve as the basis for an expanding market later on.

Whatever the reasons, the trend is clear: the Philippines is being marginalized from the dynamic flows of investment, trade, and technology that are sweeping the rest of the region. For some members of the cluster, this trend is alarming; others, however, are not sure if it is indeed negative.

Post-Cold War Regional Politics

One of the consequences of this growing marginalization is that there does not exist in the Philippines the same sensitivity to the implications of Japanese economic dominance of the region that one finds in Thailand, Indonesia, Malaysia, and Korea. So massive is the Japanese presence in Thailand, for instance, that many Thais refer to their country as a "Japanese colony." Many Asia-Pacific governments are, in fact, highly schizophrenic about the Japanese, being both desirous of Japanese investment yet apprehensive of Japanese economic might and fearful of the prospect that Japan's economic hegemony might be translated into military might.

Balancing Japanese Economic Power

It is this prospect that has led many of the Asia-Pacific political and economic elites to pressure the US to maintain a high-profile political and military presence in the region. While some hope to use US political support to gain leverage in economic negotiations with Japan, a more important goal of allying with the US is to forestall the emergence of Japan as a military power. Japan's virtual integration of the region, many of them feel, is precisely the factor that provides the impetus for remilitarization. They do not take seriously Japanese protestations of pacifism and discount fashionable statements that military might has become obsolete as a form of national power. They point instead to statements such as that of General Hiromi Kurisu, former chairman of Japan's joint chiefs of staff: "Japan needs the power to protect Japanese interest in [its neighboring] countries." They note with alacrity that Japan is now one of the world's top importers of conventional weapons, that its defense budget is now the second or third largest in the world, and that the size of its Navy is surpassed only by the Russian and US fleets. And they are ambivalent with the recent deployment of an armed "peacekeeping" expeditionary force (PKO) to Cambodia, fearing that this may legitimize future military deployments of a more imperialist nature.

Consequently, some of the same governments that are most hospitable to Japanese investment are infusing the old Cold War alliances in the Asia-Pacific region with a new content: pitting the US against Japan. Even as the Philippines was invoking the end of the Cold War to terminate the lease to the US' largest overseas bases, Singapore was concluding a deal with the Pentagon to provide US warships and planes generous access arrangements. Recently, Indonesia, Thailand, and even Malaysia, which has proposed exclusion of the US from a regional trading bloc, have come up with similar offers.

To be sure, these moves were not only motivated by a fear of Japan. They were also meant to send a message to China. But while China is a concern to some Asia-Pacific governments, its image as a "destabilizer" has been promoted mainly by unreconstructed Cold War interest groups in the West that insist on conditioning security and economic relations with China on the latter's movement toward western-style democracy. China's Asia-Pacific neighbors know, however, that while China tends to be very sensitive to border issues and to perceived threats to its sovereignty, it has usually behaved as an inwardly-turned non-expansionist power. Moreover, they view it as more or less committed to the peaceful resolution of sovereignty disputes over Taiwan, Hong Kong, and the Spratly Islands by the priority it has assigned to economic development. And they have also not failed to notice that it has accomplished post-Cold War demobilization much faster than the western powers, reducing its armed forces by some one million personnel in the late eighties.

Japan, which is seen as inherently expansionist owing to its dynamic trading economy and its elite's view of East and Southeast Asia as a natural Japanese zone of influence, is regarded as the far greater threat.

The Redefinition of Japan in US Policy

What makes the Asia-Pacific so volatile is that the US is in the midst of a historic reexamination of its Asia policy, and the Asia-Pacific elites' strategy of "using the American eagle to restrain the Japanese tiger" coincides with the agenda of an increasingly influential political current in Washington. While the State Department and the Pentagon continue to officially affirm the "strategic character" of the US-Japan alliance, there is a groping corps of trade officials, Pentagon technocrats, protectionist Congresspeople, CIA officials in search of a post-Cold War mission, and industrial policy intellectuals that are moving toward a view of Japan as the US' "strategic antagonist." These strategic elites have pushed hard to get the United States to maintain a strong economic presence in the Asia-Pacific. In fact, they have had to press a reluctant US corporate establishment, which would much rather retreat to a protected Fortress America, to aggressively dispute Japan's domination of both its home market and the regional Asia-Pacific market.

Not surprisingly, the view of these elites has found resonance within US Pacific Command, which is increasingly uneasy about the fact that the main result of its successfully fulfilling its role of "repelling Communism" in Asia has been to deliver the region to the economic hegemony of Japan. To many US officers, it is unlikely and unhistorical to imagine that the worsening economic relations and increasingly bitter technological competition between the US and Japan will not spill over to the political and military arena.

Thus, the US military's distrust of Japan that was repressed in the interest of the anti-communist alliance during the Cold War is returning to the surface. The most dramatic manifestation of this attitude was Major General Henry Stackpole's candid justification for the 48,000 US troops in Japan when he served as commander of Marine forces in that country in 1990. Already, he claimed, the Japanese have "achieved the Greater East Asia Co-Prosperity Sphere economically, without guns." This was all the more reason why "No one wants a rearmed, resurgent Japan. So we are the cap in the bottle, if you will."

Thus, in place of the Cold War divide, a more complex balance-of-power politics, with multiple key actors, is emerging in the Asia-Pacific. It is a trend that provokes a sense of deja vu in many people, a deep-seated fear that balance-of-power politics is a dangerous and unpredictable game that could produce not stability but the same uncontrollable dynamics that led to the Pacific War earlier in this century.

The Defining Conflict

To be sure, there are other sources of political instability in the region. Contrary to portrayals of the Asia-Pacific as "a region that is at peace with itself," the area is rife with tensions, antagonisms, and potential, knife-edged conflict situations. There are, for instance, conflicts stemming from continued colonialism in the region, such as struggles against French rule in New Caledonia; bitter face-offs that are a legacy of the Cold War, as in Cambodia and Korea; and conflicts over natural resources, like the Spratly Islands dispute,which are likely to be the wave of the future as prospects for oil discoveries and advances in seabed mining technology make exploitation of the South China Sea more attractive. However, in our view, in the absence of popular intervention to build a new system of regional security, the worsening US-Japan relationship is likely to be defining conflict in the Asia-Pacific in the next few decades.

A Progressive Agenda for the Region

The economic hegemony of Japan and the growing political conflict between Japan and the US are the two strategic concerns that must frame the regional agenda of the Philippine progressive movement. But the most immediate problem that must be addressed by a progressive agenda is the growing marginalization of the Philippines from the investment, trade, and technology flows in the Asia-Pacific region.

Reversing this condition entails, first of all, a major effort to redefine popular consciousness away from its continuing excessive orientation toward the United States and to anchor it in the reality that the Philippines is part of Asia. Among progressives, it is important to decisively end the traditional fixation of the left on U.S imperialism and begin a creative intellectual engagement with the regional realities that have become central determinants of the constraints as well as possibilities for Philippine development.

Second, while the threat of Japanese economic imperialism to the Philippines cannot be dismissed, there are members of the group who feel that marginalization, rather than imperialist exploitation, is currently the main problem in the Philippines' relationship with external economic powers, particularly Japan. They therefore propose that we revise our traditional approach toward foreign capital, particularly Japanese investment. Rather than oppose foreign investment in a blanket fashion, they advocate attracting the right kinds of investment and right types of investors. They note that while foreign investment is not the most strategic factor in national development, it can nevertheless help develop an economy, create jobs, and, most important, bring in much-needed technology; it all depends on the foreign investment regime. And they see as central to a progressive economic development strategy the formulation of a foreign investment policy that would maximize the positive effects of investment (developing difficult sectors of the economy like high-technology, creating jobs, and bringing in much-needed technology) and radically minimize possible negative impacts (destruction of the environment, excessive repatriation of profits, absence of technology transfer).

An Asia-Pacific Technoeconomic Bloc

This discussion of the importance of an effective foreign investment regime for the Philippines brings us right to the need for a framework of regional cooperation that would assist in making such national policies effective.

The massive economic power of Japan in the region necessitates the formation of a bloc by the weaker, subordinate economies to counter the negative exercise of that power, promote a more equitable relationship between them and Japan, and pursue long-term policies that would lessen their technological dependence on Japan.

This proposal for an "Asia-Pacific Technoeconomic Bloc" diverges from two current proposals for regional economic cooperation, APEC and EAEG. APEC, or Asia-Pacific Economic Cooperation, is really a vehicle to shore up US economic presence in the region and promote the joint domination of the Asia-Pacific by the US and Japan. EAEG, or East Asia Economic Group, which is proposed by Malaysia's Mahathir, would exclude the US from a regional bloc but hand over leadership to Japan.

An Asia-Pacific Techno-trading Bloc would also go beyond the narrow confines of the "free trade area" (AFTA) that is in the process of being established by the Association of Southeast Asian Nations (ASEAN). Merely lowering or abolishing tariffs could, in fact, be counterproductive, from the point of view of strengthening regional economic autonomy. As a Japanese analyst has pointed out, AFTA is "not worrisome" to the Japanese since it would bring about lower tariffs for products manufactured and traded within the area by Japanese firms.

The proposal envisions a more activist formation that would engage in both defensive and forward-looking actions. Defensively, such a regional formation would aim at neutralizing the now overwhelming Japanese dominance by bringing the 20 or so sovereign Asia-Pacific countries to unified positions on matters such as environmental regulation, labor rights, and technology transfer. A common labor code and common environmental code would make it difficult for runaway shops and runaway polluters from Japan and other countries to extract maximum advantage from one Asia-Pacific country by threatening to transfer their operations to another. An environmental code is especially pressing given the central role played by Japanese companies in the deforestation of Southeast Asia and Indochina, and the equally central role played by Japanese corporations in transferring pollution-intensive industries to Southeast Asia.

Similarly, a unified policy would provide powerful leverage in negotiations with Japan to transfer selected high technologies to the region — a request it can now ignore because it comes from individual firms or, more rarely, from individual governments.

But more critical would be the forward-looking, strategic cooperation aimed at changing the economic balance of power in the region. This would especially be necessary in high-tech development. Owing to the tremendous capital and research-and-development requirements and each country's still limited technical pool, the development of strategic high-technology industries such as transport equipment, machine tools, computers, and semiconductors must be pursued as a regional, Asia-Pacific-wide industrialization strategy. This would mean not only joint efforts in strategic planning, raising capital, and research and development, but also developing a plan of equitably dispersing industrial sectors through the region to extract maximum locational advantages for sector development while still benefiting local economies.

In this regard, initial divisions of labor could be based on existing complementarities: for instance, the Philippines produces many skilled computer programmers and software specialists but has rudimentary capabilities when it comes to producing computer hardware. Korea, in contrast, is relatively strong in computer hardware but weak in software development. Instead of serving as cheap labor for US data-processing firms, as they do now, Filipino programmers could be designing programs for Korean computer hardware as part of a comprehensive long-term agreement that would involve the transfer of hardware know-how to the Philippines.

Joint planning, pooling of resources, and research could also be the key to breakthroughs in the development of appropriate technologies, particularly in creating alternatives to environmentally destructive technologies, such as chemical-intensive, Green Revolution agro-technology.

Care must be taken, however, that, in contrast to the Japanese and US paradigm of corporation-driven growth, initial divisions of labor agreed upon are not allowed to congeal into permanent cleavages between countries and that technological know-how is not monopolized but systematically spread around among members of the bloc.

An Alternative Security System

Japanese economic hegemony is one of the two principal problems that must be addressed by the regional community, the other is the threat to regional peace posed by the US - Japan rivalry, Japanese rearmament, conflicts over natural resources, and persisting tensions from the Cold War and colonial eras.

A progressive agenda for the region must therefore include the creation of a system of regional security that would supersede the anachronistic Cold War bilateral and trilateral alliances constructed by the US, which are now being transformed, as noted earlier, into anti-Japanese alliances.

An immediate objective of an Alternative Security System would be to move regional conflicts from resolution by force to resolution by diplomacy. Thus, mechanisms must be evolved for pressing regional confrontations such as the Korean peninsula standoff, the continuing civil war in Cambodia, and the Spratly Islands dispute which involves the Philippines as a central actor.

The strategic goal of such a multilateral security system, however, would be more far-reaching: to move the region towards total denuclearization and significant demilitarization, which are the only guarantees of long-term peace and stability in the region. It would institute, among other things, a ban on nuclear testing in the Pacific; a prohibition on the storage and movement of nuclear arms in the region; a ban on chemical and biological weapons; withdrawal of all foreign bases from the Western Pacific; pullout of US troops from the Korean peninsula, accompanied by major cuts in the size of both the South Korean and North Korean armies; significant reductions in all other standing armies, navies, and air forces in the region; a ban on research and development of high-tech nuclear, biological, and chemical weaponry; and tight limits on the transfer of conventional arms via sales or aid.

An alternative security system for the region would build on successful limited initiatives at the subregional level during the 1980s, which were propelled by unorthodox alliances between governments, non-governmental organizations (NGOs), and mass movements in the context of favorable public opinion. Most notable have been the creation of the South Nuclear-Free Zone by 11 states; the banning of nuclear-armed and nuclear-powered vessels from New Zealand ports; and the Philippines' decision to terminate the US lease to Subic Naval Base. So strong, in fact, is the popular mood in favor of arms control in the region that even Indonesia and Malaysia, two conservative US allies, have proposed making Southeast Asia a nuclear-free zone.

The US military will resist any attempt to limit its ability to unilaterally deploy force in what it considers its God-given zone of strategic influence. But the questioning of the size and mission of the US Pacific Command going on in Washington and the fears, hopes, and fluidity let loose by the end of the Cold War in Asia have combined to open an unprecedented window of opportunity for creating a constituency for a new regional security order.

A Regional Congress of NGOs

A new Asia-Pacific order would be woefully incomplete without providing a space for institutions that allow citizens of the region to directly impact on political and economic decisionmaking.

The Asia-Pacific boasts a tremendous number and rich variety of NGOs and people's organizations. As noted above, NGOs were central actors in some of the successful demilitarization and denuclearization initiatives of the last few years. In some areas, in fact, NGOs have become as influential as political parties, economic organizations, or government bodies. Bringing together these actors into a "Regional Congress of NGOs" would create a powerful counterbalance to three extremely powerful actors: regional governments, Japan, and the US Indeed, the ability of the NGOs to transcend their specialized or national concerns, says one Pacific specialist, "may well prove to be the single most important contribution to a more habitable future for the peoples of Asia and the Pacific."

One of the key objectives of the NGO Congress would be to bring regional NGO power to bear on national efforts to promote objectives to which local elites, as well as foreign actors, are often hostile or indifferent to: protection of basic human rights, spread of democratic government, agrarian reform, protection of environment, promotion of women's rights, and defense of indigenous peoples and minorities.

Another key aim of the Congress would be to intervene in the relationship between local governments and big powers, to blunt the often negative impact of relationships based on realpolitik. In the area of human rights and environmental protection, Asia-Pacific

NGO's organizing on a regional and international basis have already had successes in isolating repressive regimes, such as the Burmese military and the Marcos dictatorship, or making it difficult for others, like the Suharto government, to get away with shooting demonstrators.

This experience can be profitably extended to the area of foreign aid. With Japan becoming the region's prime aid donor, the Japanese are now debating the nature, thrust, and delivery of foreign aid. And there is a growing body of domestic opinion critical of the close relationship between Japanese aid policy and the objectives of Japanese corporations and the methods of aid delivery.

Organized nationwide, Asia-Pacific NGOs can more effectively intervene in this debate and gain more control over the process of delivery of Japanese aid, which has often enriched local elites while advancing infrastructure projects designed to support the activities of Japanese corporations. The result could be arrangements in which the Japanese government is obligated to clear aid projects with the regional NGO Congress and local NGOs, and the latter's views are made central to the delivery, maintenance, and evaluation of approved projects.

Conclusion

The end of the Cold War has initiated a fluid period in the Asia-Pacific. The fate of the Philippines is now inescapably bound with the future of the region; and that the future of the region could very well be marked by irreversible Japanese economic hegemony and worsening military and political relations between Japan and the United States. With popular intervention, however, the future of the region can be different. The foregoing pages have laid out an alternative future with three pillars: an Asia-Pacific Technoeconomic Bloc, an Alternative Security System, and a Regional Congress of NGOs.

ABOUT CIVICUS

Mission

CIVICUS is an international alliance of organizations and individuals *to strengthen citizen action and influence throughout the world* through voluntary initiatives, philanthropy and community service.

Overview

CIVICUS is uniquely different from any other international body. CIVICUS:

❖ includes both donor and donee organizations;
❖ includes a broad cross-section of the third sector (voluntary initiatives, philanthropy, community service, etc.);
❖ is global in nature;
❖ complements what governments achieve because governments alone cannot manage the complex relationships among and within communities and nations;
❖ promotes regional efforts by generating global, moral, technical and legal support; and
❖ informs governments and encourages people, communities and organizations attempting to increase citizen participation and influence.

Goals

CIVICUS is intended to be an international forum in which regional, national and local citizen organizations can exchange knowledge and experience. CIVICUS will:

❖ Encourage regional and national associations whose purpose is to strengthen local efforts for involvement and citizen influence.

❖ Help establish an international climate that will provide global, moral, technical and legal support to those trying to develop pluralism and empowerment in their countries and communities.

Priority Program Activities

❖ Serve as a resource for helpful information and contacts.
❖ Implement a three-part project consisting of:

- an **Action Report** on the growing impact of citizens on local and global problems and aspirations;
- a **World Assembly** in January 1995 to present the report and secure members' insights for future strategy; and
- a **follow-up strategy** to accelerate the trend.

❖ Identify examples of innovative and inspiring projects for possible replication or adaption.
❖ Provide moral support and facilitate access to technical and legal assistance to regions.

Board of Directors

The board of directors may total as many as 36 members. However, the 20-member Founding Board is comprised of representatives from six continents, all of whom are active in citizen involvement. The list includes:

Farida Allaghi (Co-chairperson)
Arab Gulf Programme
for the United Nations Development Organizations
Riyadh, Saudi Arabia

Mohammed Barakat
Social Welfare Institutions
National Council for Social Services
Arab Conference for NGOs
Beirut, Lebanon

Margaret Bell
International Association for Volunteer Effort
Sydney, Australia

Tim Brodhead
J.W. McConnell Family Foundation
Montreal, Canada

Miguel Darcy de Oliveira (Co-chairperson)
Instituto de Acão Cultural (IDAC)
Rio de Janeiro, Brazil

Khadija Cherif
Ligue Tunisienne des droits de l'Homme
Bureau d'Internet Canada Universite d'Ottawa
Tunis, Tunisia

Eddah Wacheke Gachukia
The Forum for African Women Educationalists
Nairobi, Kenya

Marcela Gajardo
Facultad Latinamericana de Ciencias Sociales
Santiago, Chile

Ricardo Govela
Centro Mexicano para la Filantropía
Mexico City, Mexico

Milad Hanna
Supreme Council of Culture
Tawlik Coptic Society
Housing Committee, Peoples Assembly
Cairo, Egypt

James A. Joseph
Council on Foundations
Washington, D.C., United States

Graça Machel (Co-chairperson)
Association for Community Development
Maputo, Mozambique

Miklos Marschall
Deputy Mayor
Budapest, Hungary

Carlos A. Monjardino (Co-chairperson)
Fundacão Oriente
Lisbon, Portugal

Cuca Robledo Montecel
Intercultural Development Research Association
San Antonio, Texas, United States

Horacio R. Morales
Philippine Rural Reconstruction Movement (PRRM)
Quezon City, Philippines

Brian O'Connell (Co-chairperson)
INDEPENDENT SECTOR
WAshington, D.C., United States

Gerard Pantin
Service Volunteered for All (SERVOL)
Port-of-Spain, Trinidad

Rajesh Tandon
Society for Participatory Research in Asia (PRIA)
New Delhi, India

Sylvie Tsyboula
Fondation de France
Paris, France

Secretariat

Sandra Trice Gray
Vice President, International Initiatives
INDEPENDENT SECTOR

Theresa Siegl
Assistant Director, International Initiatives
INDEPENDENT SECTOR

William Dietel
Consultant
(Former President, Rockefeller Brothers Fund)

ABOUT THE AUTHOR

Isagani R. Serrano is Vice President of the Philippine Rural Reconstruction Movement (PRRM) and works on development policy and advocacy.

He has been involved in people's movements since he became a peace activist in mid-1960s. His participation in the resistance against the Marcos dictatorship cost him seven years in prison.

His works include a collection of essays on environment and development, *Pay Now, Not Later* (1994), *On Civil Society* (1993), and a poetry collection, *Firetree* (1985). He also co-authored *Bataan: A Case on Ecosystem Approach to Sustainable Development in the Philippines* (1991).

Serrano has been working for CIVICUS since the Budapest meeting in March 1993.

A NOTE ON THE TYPE

The text of this book was set via a 486-DX2-66 computer and a Linotronic 200 output device using Aldus PageMaker 5.0 for page composition and layout. It was set in the digitized version of Galliard Roman, a type designed by Matthew Carter in 1978 based on the roman type cut in 1568 by French typefounder Robert Granjon.

Book and cover design by Fidel Rillo / Paragraphics®
Printed and bound in the Philippines by Raintree Publishing, Inc.